A Country Twelvemonth

The country life can be magical for young children

A Country Twelvemonth

FRED ARCHER

ALAN SUTTON

First published in the United Kingdom in 1992 by
Alan Sutton Publishing Limited
Phoenix Mill · Far Thrupp · Stroud · Gloucestershire

First published in the United States of America in 1993 by
Alan Sutton Publishing Inc · Wolfeboro Falls · NH 03896–0848

British Library Cataloguing in Publication Data

A catalogue record for this book is available from
the British Library

ISBN 07509-0268-X

Library of Congress Cataloging in Publication Data applied for

Photographs: The Museum of English Rural Life Reading.

Edited by John Hudson.

Typeset in 10/14 Bembo.
Typesetting and origination by
Alan Sutton Publishing Limited.
Printed in Great Britain by
The Bath Press, Avon.

Contents

Introduction

Today, Fred Archer lives in contented retirement near the sea in Devon, some way removed from the land-locked Worcestershire village he has immortalized in book after book since first breaking into print with *The Distant Scene* at the age of fifty-two. That was back in 1967, and his reputation as one of England's best-read and best-loved country writers is founded upon a remarkable spell of creativity for a decade after that, when he produced successful books at the rate of almost one a year.

From the start, critics of perception and sensitivity saw in his work something beyond the commonplace. They liked his lack of pretension and sentimentality: 'His writing goes a long way to restoring some of the right kind of robustness to the recent past,' wrote *The Countryman*'s reviewer, while Auberon Waugh hailed him as 'the true voice of the livelier English peasantry'. But Waugh was perhaps closer to the essential Archer when he wrote: 'His reminiscences of country life really do have humour, poetry and a curious literary perception of their own,' and Ralph Wightman awarded him the ultimate country writer's accolade when he declared that his characters were as real as Thomas Hardy's. It is interesting that while Archer is an admirer of Hardy he is even more conscious of the work of another Dorset writer of Victorian times, William Barnes, who wrote *Linden Lea* and a great deal of deceptively artless dialect verse besides. It would be wrong to suggest that there are endless parallels between Archer and Barnes, but they do have in common the 'curious literary perception' of which Waugh wrote. There is much more scholarship, skill and learning in both of them than is superficially apparent, and the same can be said of another writer for whom Archer has great admiration, A.G. Street.

Fred Archer's path to authorship began in 1966, when he was still farming in Ashton-under-Hill, and still in contact, albeit in their old age, with some of the characters who spring again to life on these pages. He was involved in a car accident in Cheltenham that resulted in a whiplash injury to his neck, and during his enforced inactivity he was persuaded to give a talk to members of the local Methodist Guild. In the spirit of many such a venture, it was entitled Farm, Field and Fireside. And in the spirit of many a grateful club official on such occasions, the Methodist Guild's secretary enthused: 'That was good. You ought to write a book.' Where the story differs is that in this case, with nothing more strenuous to occupy him, that is exactly what Fred Archer proceeded to do, in spite of boyhood memories of painfully low marks for spelling and punctuation.

And this is where fate took a hand. The number one literary celebrity in the area of Bredon Hill and for a great many miles beyond was John Moore, a now somewhat neglected but at that time acclaimed country writer. One day, when Archer was some ten thousand words into his fledgling book, he received a letter from Moore out of the blue, asking him where he could find a badger sett so that he and a group of students could watch the creatures in their natural environment. When they met, Archer took his manuscript along with him – and it was with John Moore's encouragement and through his practical help in contacting publishers that The Distant Scene was accepted by Hodder and Stoughton. This was after the book had been rejected by three other publishers, and there was another major setback before it finally appeared in the bookshops. 'When I received my first proof copies, I took one of them down to Kemerton for John Moore but found that he had been admitted to hospital that day,' says Archer. 'Three days later I received the sad news that he had died.'

The flurry of literary activity that followed over the next few years saw the end of Fred Archer the farmer, and his break with the village that fuelled his creative fires. Domestically and in terms of health they were times of upheaval, but when in his mind he retreated to the Worcestershire countryside of his childhood, his evocations of those distant days were still pin-sharp, affectionate and free from affectation. The impression today is that he feels more at home in a part of Devon thickly populated by comparative newcomers like himself and his wife Elsie than in Ashton-under-Hill, now 'gentrified' almost beyond recognition from the community of his youth. It is scarcely a village with mud on its boots these days.

Archer's greatest gift is as a listener and observer. Auberon Waugh's allusion to his being 'the true voice of the livelier English peasantry' will do as a thumb-nail sketch, and with his rich Worcestershire brogue it was one with which Fred Archer did not feel inclined to quibble during his several years as a successful after-dinner speaker and radio and TV personality. But his true status in his home village was that of the privately, though not extensively, educated son of a dynamic, self-made and very comfortably-off landowner and farmer, an astute businessman with an eye for a gimmick long before anyone knew the meaning of the word; what made young Fred special was his ear for the talk and his feel for the rhythm of life of the men of the land around him, the carter and the shepherd and the cottager, and in this he did indeed capture the essence of what a class-conscious writer like Waugh would see as the peasantry.

The carousel has slowed down a little since the days when he was on TV talking to Samantha Fox in a horse trough, or singing with a pig in Selfridge's in Oxford Street to promote his latest book. 'The things people will do for money,' the lugubrious and wry Ted Moult remarked to him, perhaps reflecting on his own standing at the time as the nation's most unlikely double glazing salesman. Maybe both men, at that moment, pondered upon how far they had travelled from their roots on the land. But unlike the unhappy Moult, Archer knew where he had been and where he was going; and when he eventually split from Hodder – 'They said they'd found another author called Archer, and one was enough' – there was no shortage of others anxious to harness his talents.

A neighbour of John Moore, a soul mate of Barnes, an admirer of writers as diverse as Matthew Arnold, Hardy, John Clare and that myriad of long-ago 'Anons' who dreamed up country lore rhymes about red skies at night and casting clouts; Fred Archer is all of these, and he is ever-mindful, too, of another South Midlands boy from just up the Avon at Stratford who wrote a play or two when the first Elizabeth was Queen. Not many people mention him in the same breath as Will Shakespeare, and that is as it should be; but Archer has no hesitation in drawing parallels between the banter of his companions in the fields of sixty years ago and the speech patterns of the Bard, and that startling juxtaposition says much about the originality and surprise element of his thinking. It tells us that Fred Archer is his own man, and he is fun, so cast aside all thoughts of Shakespeare and Barnes and poor old mad John Clare, and simply sit back and enjoy some of the best country writing you have read 'since Adam was a bwoy'.

John Hudson
Gloucestershire, 1992

CHAPTER ONE

January

The Shepherd and the World Sprout Champion

January, and so many memories of my young days on the farm are bound up with the feeding of animals. Labour was cheap then, and the cowman Tom Whittle and I devoted so much time to this task, whole days, it seemed, at this time of year. We always fed what was known as bait to the milking cows and yarded cattle, a mixture of chaff, pulped mangolds and ground oats. The chaff was cut once a week by a chaff-cutter in the barn. Mangolds were pulped every day, while the oats were ground by the miller at Sedgeberrow water mill on the little river Isbourne. The chaff was raked out from under the loft into a big heap in the middle of the barn, and the mangold pulp was shovelled over it. The ground oats were then scattered on top, and Tom and I would face each other and mix the feed with shovels. It was made a day in advance, and it was slightly warm the following day when the skips were filled ready for carrying to the cattle.

One cold morning the Rushton Hornsby oil engine that turned the pulley wheels for the pulping and chaff-cutting took some time to start. We eventually got it going by heating the vaporizer with a blowlamp until it was red hot. It certainly did the job, but rather too well, and before we knew it the engine was racing at far faster a speed than usual, and the whole barn was rattling. 'Let's have it, bwoy,' Tom shouted. 'It's not often the engine goes so well as this!' The racing cutter chopped the fodder as fast as we could feed it in, but after a little while even we had to admit that it was all getting a bit out of hand. I climbed down from the loft and pulled at the exhaust valve lever to cut out the engine; the great flywheels were revolving at a frightening speed, but at last the machinery ground to a halt. It was clear that the flywheel had slipped along its scale almost to the end, and that it would have flown off if it had been left to run a few more seconds. I wondered where it would have landed, and imagined it careering across the yard, causing untold damage. Anyway, that was one day when the chaff was cut in record time!

The calves and milking cows also had their daily ration of cattle cake. We kibbled these corrugated slabs in the cake-crusher in the granary, mixing half linseed cake with half cotton; the little calves had linseed cake on its own. Tom cut the hay from the ricks with a heavy hay knife, and it always gave us a pleasant smell of summer, even in January. My job was to take a fork and carry the hay to the cattle in the yard. After lunch, Tom and I walked to the top of Bredon Hill, where forty half-bred Herefords wintered out on the slopes. Turpin the carthorse shared their field, and we harnessed him to a muck cart standing beside the rick on the hill; we filled it with hay, and I then led the horse in a straight line across the bare winter land, and the cattle followed us as Tom pitched the hay from the cart. What a fine sight in winter, the cows contentedly eating hay on the frosty hill. After Turpin had fed, too, we left the cart back beside the rick and walked down the hill for dinner. As we approached the Plough and Harrow Tom said: 'I'm going to have a pint of cider,' a reward he had well earned. I left him there, and when we met up again after dinner we fed the cattle in the yards once more, and suckled the young calves on the nurse cows. Up to three calves could be placed on a newly-calved animal. This daily round went on until May Day, when the cattle were once again put out to grass, and though it was hard work, it taught me much. Tom was a good stockman to work under, one who knew his animals and was quick to detect any that were not thriving.

The same could be said – only more so – for Alf Tidmarsh, our shepherd, a man blessed with so many of the finer characteristics associated with his calling. In Elizabethan times shepherds were renowned for being merry, piping fellows. An old rhyme goes:

> I heard a mess of merry shepherds sing
> A joyful song full of sweet delight.

Professor L.P. Jacks, who for some years lived in the Worcestershire village of Grafton, near Beckford, studied the ways of shepherds on Bredon Hill. Dad knew him quite well before the First World War. His book *Mad Shepherds* had an atmosphere all of its own, and in it he wrote about Snarley Bob, Bredon Hill's legendary shepherd. I knew Snarley Bob, or should I say I knew the man Professor Jacks had in mind when he wrote about him. He worked a little further round the hill from my village of Ashton-under-Hill. Shepherds are a race apart; they are solitary individuals bent over their crooks as they look after their flocks. A shepherd must be a patient man who waits; he must stand and stare. A galloping shepherd is a bad man among sheep, for he will miss the ewe that has been struck by the fly. He will miss seeing the ewe that is overdue at lambing, or the ewe that lambs and has no milk, with her lamb sucking continually to no avail.

I like 'The Scholar-Gypsy', by Matthew Arnold, which starts:

> Go, for they call you, Shepherd, from the hill;
> Go, Shepherd, and untie the wattled cotes:
> No longer leave thy wistful flock unfed,
> Nor let thy bawling fellows rack their throats,
> Nor the cropp'd herbage shoot another head.
> But when the fields are still,
> And the tired men and dogs all gone to rest,
> And only the white sheep are sometimes seen
> Cross and recross the strips of moon-blanch'd green,
> Come, Shepherd, and again renew the quest!

January is often a vital month for shepherds. It is true the majority of lambs are born in February and March, but the shepherd of a pedigree flock breeds from his ewes so that they lamb down in January. The young ram lambs will have longer to grow and will be able to be used for mating ewes in the October following. My Dorset Horn ewes used to lamb in October to breed early lambs for the spring trade. Dorset Horns are one of a few breeds that will mate with the ram in May and lamb in October. Most ewes won't show any interest in the ram until the shortening days of September and October. In

The sheep safe in lowland pastures in the hard months

the spring, a young ram's fancy doesn't turn to thoughts of love – not until the autumn.

In January the shepherd must keep an eye on all the in-lamb ewes. Being heavy in lamb and often with wet fleeces, they easily get cast on their flat backs in a furrow or even on level ground, so to avoid casualties he must look at his flock at least twice a day. He feeds his animals with discretion: not too much bulky food, but a diet of concentrates. A heavy meal of mangolds or kale can upset the ewe to the point where she has a prolapse – what was commonly known as putting out her wether. I spent a lot of my childhood days with Alf Tidmarsh, a shepherd with a sort of superior air about him. No ordinary farm labourer was Alf. He didn't come to the barn for his orders every morning like other men, striking one and all as much more of a law unto himself. A.G. Street used to write about how careful a farmer had to be to enlist the shepherd of the farm to come to help with the haymaking. Yes, one had to be diplomatic, impressing on the shepherd that no one could build a hay rick like he could, and that the work could not possibly proceed without him. It was right that a man of such talents should be respected.

Shepherd Alf was such a man. His lambing pen in the barn was his private work place. No one intruded apart from the farmer, and here he practised the art and mystery of shepherding. Dressed in a sacking overall like a pinafore frock, he resembled what I thought was another Moses, except that Moses's would be a musical pipe while Alf's short clay tobacco burner, known as a nose-warmer, sat almost permanently between his gold-stained moustache and his bottom lip. Many were the January mornings that I saw him descend Bredon Hill with the hoar frost white on his sacking smock, and he seemed to propel himself along as if his crook were a third leg. His corduroy fall-fronted trousers were yorked below the knee with leather straps, and his boots were always well dubbined and a cut above the farmworkers' hobnails. He was one of Nature's gentlemen, blending with the surrounding countryside and looking so much a part of the rural scene. With the engine-driven shearing machine and men with wide cutters in the New Zealand style, shearing hundreds of sheep a day, it is now a far cry from the times when I saw Alf on the shearing floor in the barn. I hardly dared look through the partly-opened doors in case I startled one of the ewes. The big man wrestled with his sheep on the floor as the hand-shearer clipped the milk-white wool. It would be ten to twelve minutes before the ewe, stripped of her fleece, rejoined the flock.

Shepherds and their sheep are, of course, commonplace in the Bible. Quotations such as the one from Isaiah – 'All ye like sheep have gone astray' – allude to nature, the way flocks break through hedges and jump the walls of their fields, but of all the figures of speech the Bible has made familiar, none is stranger than 'the Lamb of God'. We have forgotten the original Hebrew context, the burnt offering of a lamb to God, and the phrase has been lifted to express to us, beautifully and strangely through a timid and somewhat stupid animal, the concept of courage and gentleness. Perhaps when the Glasgow Orpheus Choir sings 'All in an April Evening', with its references to the little lambs and the Lamb of God, it all falls into place; but it is not what was originally intended.

Shearing before the advent of machines

Another fine old country character I think of at this time of year is George Hunting, a cousin of mine and a real native of our village who still reigns, in my book at least, as the Champion Sprout Picker of the World. It all started one cold January day in the 1930s when my Dad and his partner Harry Bailey rented a field from Harry Roberts of Great Washbourne, just over the border in Gloucestershire. Mr Roberts used to farm in the traditional way, fattening his lambs on turnips which made them grow almost as high as the hurdles that formed their pens, and his sheep had cleared the ground shortly before my father and Mr Bailey moved in to put it under Brussels sprouts. They had been the first to grow sprouts on Bredon Hill, developing their own excellent strain. Varieties had started to improve back in around 1911, and names like Norman Boswell, Alf Baker, R.R. Smith and Byrd Bros were all famous in the Vale for their sprout seed. Norman Boswell called his variety Rous Lench after the village in which he lived; Alf Baker was celebrated well beyond his farm on Hipton Hill; R.R. Smith's Camden strain weighed well, and though its stems were short and the sprouts were hard to pick, they were always of good quality. As for the Byrd brothers' special brand, I always thought it took some beating. The stems were tall and the sprouts were not crowded, and because of this they kept clean and easy to pick. The fact was that no one who grew sprouts commercially bought seeds from a seedsman, and there was a bizarre streak to some of the experiments. I remember one farmer cross-pollinating sprouts with red cabbage, the pickling cabbage, giving the Brussels an unusual purple hue. Unintended cross-pollination by bees was a constant problem, and when my father and Harry Bailey started experimenting on an acre at the top of Bredon Hill, they were pleased that the field was well away from other crops.

The first we heard of sprout picking as a competitive venture was when Dad came in to midday dinner one day and greeted us with the words: 'I think George will create a record today; he's aiming to pick forty pots of sprouts.' The equivalent to this in modern times is eighty nets of twenty pounds per net. At tea time he was back in his old 1913 Sunbeam tourer, his face flushed by the chill wind but beaming. 'He's done it,' he announced, as he burst in through the back door. Next day at Evesham Market, as he and Harry Bailey stood and watched their sprouts being sold by Mr Lavell, they told one or two other growers of George's great feat. 'Can't be done,' some of them replied. The news spread fast, and when it was reported in the local paper it led to a spate of letters from market gardeners, some disputing the claim, some dismissing it as a stunt to help the Archer-Bailey partnership sell more sprout seed, and others accepting that yes, it might just be possible to pick forty pots in eight hours. Eventually, Jack Hodges, a merchant and grower from Evesham, suggested a competition at Rous Lench, with a cup for the winner. Unfortunately George was ill with 'flu that day, and the prize went to a picker from Bretforton, but I remember a later occasion in 1937 when he left the rest of the field standing at the last contest at Charlton, near Evesham.

Another topcoat morning, it was, and some eighteen competitors lined up like horses before a great race. Each man had to pick for two hours, and there was a couple of women from Tardebigge, near Bromsgrove, who entered, and did pretty well. George, stripped to his waistcoat and with rolled-up sleeves, soon filled his first net, and the crackle of leaves, the noise of sprouts snapping from the stems and the chatter of the spectators soon made us forget about the cold. Jack Hodges was at the microphone, and he kept us laughing in his inimitable way as he described the scene. When the two hours had expired, each competitor, followed by a steward to make sure that he picked clean and cleared the stems, handed his nets to the officials for weighing. To judge the quality, a panel of shrewd growers and merchants took nets at random and emptied them on a market gardener's dray on the headland, checking the contents for leaves and bits of stem that would depress their market value. It came as no surprise to those of us who knew him when George Hunting's nets were voted best in both quantity and quality; I believe he picked about seventeen nets of twenty pounds each in his two hours, and his record still stands undefeated, the Sprout Picking Champion of the World. 'Beachcomber' in the *Daily Express* wrote a funny piece about it all, the BBC was there to record the occasion – and best of all, newsreel cameras made a little documentary film of the occasion. The following Saturday, the Regal cinema in Evesham was packed with folk from the Vale, not for Cary Grant or James Stewart but to watch George Hunting winning the cup at Charlton. Harry Bettridge, the legendary proprietor of the Bon Marché store in Evesham, had donated an overcoat for the winner, and he cashed in with an advertisement in the *Journal* reading: 'The Sprout Picking Champion Wears A Bon Marché Overcoat.'

I often wonder why the organizers bothered to stage such shows in those hard years, when men picked sprouts for sixpence a pot and the growers grew them for a few shillings. It was a time of odd stunts, of course, challenges and marathons, and the chance of winning a pound or so for your efforts no doubt had its appeal. I do know that more prolific strains of Brussels have been bred since those times, in spite of the fact that the sprouts themselves are smaller, and that men on the Cotswolds have picked more than a hundred nets in a day. But for me George will always be the true champion and I am proud to have picked alongside him, even if he could beat me almost two to one. I always considered him one of the real back-room boys of the Vale of Evesham, and his life story was one of hard work and complete contentment. As for his ability in picking sprouts, his secret lay in his big hands and his knack of moving his fingers very quickly. He died just before Christmas 1985, at the age of eighty-seven, and when I met him for the last time in the August of that year he still remembered that great day; and yes, he kept that silver cup to the very end, even though the Bon Marché overcoat had long since bitten the dust.

The fact that harvesting went on in January gave the lie to the thought that this was simply the dead of the year, a time in which to lie low. Better still, we could even do some planting towards the end of the month, if the earth was not frozen hard and the frost had left a sugary mould or tilth on the ploughed land. A few sacks of round-seeded and hardy early peas was the crop, planted in rows by a horse-drawn drill not unlike the one invented by Jethro Tull in around 1701. He was a church organist in Berkshire, and while he played, his mind would wander from the music; those long, symmetrical organ pipes – could something similar be adapted to plant seeds neatly in rows, so that the weeds could be controlled by the same man, and the same horse, and another implement with which to hoe in between the crops? The result was that for the next two hundred years or more, seed drilling and horse-hoeing were a vital slice of life on the arable farm. I remember, one year, doing the job with my Uncle George and a horse called Blackbird, with me leading and my uncle guiding the horse-hoe. We used Blackbird only when the best four horses were at the plough, and he was a sort of reject, an Ishmael of the tribe. He had only one eye and continually stopped between the rows making a pretence to stale, the term used when a horse passes water. Uncle George was not a patient man, and was always conscious of the acreage we had covered in a day, when my Dad or Harry Bailey asked him how we had done. After a few days the job was at last completed, and I do not know who was the most relieved, my uncle, Blackbird or me. What is certain is that the task could not have taken any longer in the times of old Jethro Tull.

CHAPTER TWO

February

Candlemas and Cold Cures

What was life really like in a country village in February three-score or more years ago? I can see in the mind's eye a picture of men going home in the fading light of the evening: John, a hedger, leaving the half-laid hedge and walking down the village street with a piece of dry hawthorn for his cottage fire. These pieces, which were put on the fire after tea and banked around with slack coal, were always called blocks rather than logs. John had a jerky step, and his hobnailed boots rang on the road like a carthorse. Then, every night at knocking-off time, the farm men who worked on Bredon Hill were loaded with sacks of coal, tins of paraffin, baskets of bread and groceries, a bag of corn for the fowls, meal for the pig. It seemed that no-one on those winter evenings went home empty-handed. 'Back-carriage pays' was a saying of the old carriers, and it applied to these farm workers, too. If the basket carried the food and drink in the morning, many's the time it carried a rabbit back off the hill at night for Wednesday's stew.

With the flickering light of a hurricane lantern, Tom turned the cows out to the meadow about six o'clock. They picked their way along the grass verge to save their feet on the flinty road, then plunged knee-deep in the quagmire of the gateway to the field. The newly calved cow bawled back to her young one in the barn. She never grazed the scanty sward, but stood knee-deep all night by the gate calling to her new-born. Sometimes she broke the fence and trotted back to the yard. After tea there was the scurry of card players making their way to the local whist drive with candle lanterns. Their chatter was a twice-weekly event in those pre-Lent days, but during the forty days and nights their sport ceased until after Easter. On dry days, when the frost-laced earth had gone into a sugary mould, George and I went to pea-drill. I led our old horse Flower up and down Finches Piece while George held the drill tails and kept the rows reasonably straight. The east wind was cutting to the face as we filled the hoppers with round-seeded Telegraph peas on the headland. Another boy followed with the harrows. How the soil dried in those cold days, I remember, and what a time it seemed before the peas came through the ground.

Our Saxon ancestors called February 'sprout kele' – kele being kele wort, now better known as colewort or potwort. Shakespeare might have had it in mind when he wrote: 'While greasy Joan doth keel the pot.'

Like our forebears, we still see February as a time of year when the stewpot is more to our tastes than the salad bowl. But more to the point with sprout kele, as far as I am concerned, is its reminder that in February those other sprouts, from Brussels, are at last giving way to purple-sprouting broccoli, the poor man's asparagus, with that special taste all of its own. Yes, it makes February a month to be welcomed, when the first shoots of broccoli can be picked – 'them purple spurters', as one old man in the village used to call the shoots when I was a boy. Their delicious taste can almost make up for the weather this month brings, the kind of intense, lingering cold that can make the old tag 'February Fill-Dyke' seem almost like wishful thinking. Torrential rain is no fun, but it is surely to be preferred, in season, to frost that can cement the ground into the third month of the year, or snow that can still plague the shepherd in the lambing pen. I have led the horse on the pea drills when the cold winds following the frost have made a brown sugar mould on the ploughland; but then again, I have seen the ground steam behind the harrows in the weak winter sun, so this can be a fickle month, too. Not that the farmers of old were pleased if the sun peeped through on 2 February. To the Christian Church that day marks the Feast of the Purification of the Virgin, but it had its significance in pagan times, too, as we are reminded in the seventeenth-century couplet:

> Tis an omen bad, the yeomen say
> If Phoebus shews his face the second day.

In the same way that we decorate our houses with ivy, holly and mistletoe at Christmas, it was the custom to replace the greenery on old Candlemas Eve, 13 February, and decorate the house with sprays of box from Valentine's Day until Easter. This, in turn, was replaced at Easter by yew, which was removed at Whitsun to give way to boughs of birch. Then came oak, green rushes and May boughs, flying in the face of another tradition that tells us that May blossom indoors is a bringer of bad luck. Herrick wrote of Valentine's Eve or old Candlemas Day:

> Down with the rosemary and bays,
> Down with the mistletoe.
> Instead of holly, now upraise
> The greener box for show.
>
> The holly hitherto did sway,
> Let box now domineer
> Until the dancing Easter Day
> On Easter's Eve appear.
>
> Then youthful box which now hath grace
> Your houses to renew,
> Grown old surrender must his place
> Unto the crisped yew.
>
> When yew is out, then birch comes in
> And many flowers beside,
> Both of a fresh and fragrant hue
> To honour Whitsuntide.
>
> Green rushes, then, and sweeter bents
> With cooler oaken boughs,
> Come in for comely ornaments
> To re-adorn the house.
>
> Thus times do shift, each thing in turn does hold;
> New things succeed as former things grow old.

Physical jerks were the doctor's orders when the temperature dropped

Despite the old saying 'As the days lengthen so the cold strengthens', birds appear on currant, pear and plum. The mistle thrush or storm cock sings, and larks soar and twitter on the clear, crisp days. On Valentine's Day the partridge is said to pair and leave the covey. Bullfinches feed on the fruit buds. It seems a shame that such a handsome bird should cause such havoc, and earn himself the name of pick-a-bud among gardeners.

Candlemas is a date in the calendar as important as any in terms of weather lore. We are told that:

> If Candlemas Day be fair and bright
> Winter will have another flight.
> If on Candlemas Day it be shower and rain
> Winter is done and will not come again.

In spirit this is very close to the saying for 2 February – if the sun is shining at this early stage of the year, be sure that you will be paying for it later on. Another rhyme tells us that:

> The farmer should have on Candlemas Day
> Half his straw and half his hay.

And according to yet another couplet:

> You should on Candlemas Day
> Throw candles and candlesticks away.

I must say I am intrigued by this last one, for it tells us much about the rhythm and pattern of our forefathers' lives. It implies that only in the very dead of the year are the days short enough to warrant the expense of sitting up by artificial light, and that by mid-February the time has come to let nature alone dictate the pattern of your going to bed and rising. Since it is dark long before mid-evening at this time of year, that would suggest some fairly early nights, and it is indeed the case that our grandfathers groped to bed with little light after resting by the flicker of the fire at the end of the day. I know my grandfather would wind the long-case clock at nine o'clock, and if visitors lingered he would hold open the door for them and wish them goodnight. But winter's back does usually break in about the middle of February, and there are increasing signs that spring is on the way as the snowdrops or Candlemas bells cheer us, and white turns to gold when the crocuses peep cautiously through the warm soil and the round-bellied ewes take more room at the trough.

In the Vale of Evesham, I still cannot think of this time without recollections of the town's Candlemas Fair, once a great horse event but more recently mainly a sale of some of the best store cattle in the Midlands. As a small boy at school I rushed through my sandwich lunch and ran to the market to watch the sale of the cart horses, the great black giants of the Midlands, along with the nags and ponies. For one day Evesham seemed full of horses, full of breeched and gaitered men carrying whips. There were carters with five-year-old shires being offered for town work, sound in wind and limb and good workers in all gears. As these faithful shiny-coated, feathery-hooved farm horses were put through their paces, little men tugged at their halters. Dad told me it was good policy for chaps built like jockeys to lead them through the ring, as it made them look so much bigger. Horse copers or dealers descended on Evesham from the big Midlands towns on the lookout for good animals aged about five to pull railway drays or brewers' waggons, and when they fancied one they would say: 'Give a run, carter.' The carter would then trot the horse up and down the High Street, and it would be vetted for defects in wind and bone. Most of the horses were specially 'got up for sale', their tails plaited with straw and their manes decorated with red, white and blue ribbons.

I envied everyone who bought a pony, since for years it had been my ambition to own and ride one. One Candlemas I had put together five pounds in savings certificates, and so at last I persuaded Dad to let me take the plunge. A pound a leg, Kitty cost me, and a youth called Bert who worked for us rode her home bareback through the darkness of that Candlemas night. She gave that strong young rider no problems, but she had a hard mouth, and when I tried her up on Bredon Hill I could not stop her. My dreams were squashed, and after keeping her another winter, Dad sold her to some gypsies for the price I had paid for her. It is for Kitty and the fair, though, that I best remember Candlemas, that and the pea-drilling in the first week of February, with the familiar 'ker-wit' cry of the partridges as they took shelter for the night in the furrows. It was a sound I often heard as we unhitched our mare Flower from her burden as dusk ended our labours for the day.

Another man who was never short of work in this month of 'flu, colds and snuffles was our village doctor, Edward Roberson, one of those pillars of society who was also chairman of the parish council and the school board, a guardian of the poor and I do not know what else. Picture a man with a closely cropped beard, a frock coat and a box hat – a figure not unlike Edward VII – who drove through the village in a trap pulled by a cob called Lavender. He kept no surgery hours, but was on call at all times except when haymaking or shooting partridge on his small farm.

And I mean it when I say 'at all times'. In fact he made a point of visiting his patients at night, when he said they were 'at their worst'. One time, our cowman's mother was taken ill with pneumonia, a killer in those days, and Dr Roberson arrived late on a Sunday evening. 'She needs poulticing, and I have no linseed meal,' he said.

'We have some linseed in the barn, but it's not ground into meal,' the cowman replied.

It was their only chance, however, and that is why the two men were to be found with a blowlamp at midnight starting the Rushton Hornsby oil engine to belt-drive the mill for grinding linseed. 'Do half a hundred-weight, Tom,' the doctor ordered. 'There's 'flu about, and someone else might get pneumonia.' They ground the meal into the early hours, taking time off only to poultice Tom's mother. She got well again; all his patients seemed to. The medicine he dispensed in those days was vile to taste, sometimes turning the tablespoon green, but it fixed the inner man.

I can still picture our GP mixing his medicine in the surgery – no frock coat and topper here, but a velvet jacket and smoking cap. So many spots of this, so many of that. . . . The cloudy sediment went to the bottom of the bottles, which were then corked, wrapped and finally secured with red sealing wax. 'Give it a thundering good shake before you take it,' he always said as he handed the mixture down from his shelf. But he was so much more than a dispenser of potions and a fixer of bones. He was a kind of village wise man. Folk went to him in his role as a guardian for parish relief and he filled in their pension forms. As chairman of the school governors Dr Roberson searched heads for nits and kept a close watch on the temperature in the classroom with his thermometer; 40 degrees Fahrenheit, and plenty of physical exercise and singing was the order of the day; and once, when the mercury showed freezing point, he sent everybody home, an enlightened attitude in those days. Chairman of the Sick and Dividend Society, he vetted would-be claimants in his little room by the front door. Club members recalled that the curtains were not always drawn properly, and village lads would peep in, laughing, as the old doctor examined them by candlelight, sometimes dropping hot wax on their naked bodies. Perhaps it was because of these less-than-ideal conditions that his diagnoses were sometimes a little off the mark. When he was examining Tom Hunting for membership of the sick club, he pronounced that he had suffered from rheumatic fever.

'Yes,' replied Tom. 'I got it in the trenches. How do you know?'

'Just a flutter in your heart,' the doctor replied, and Tom used to laugh as he grew older and older and his heart kept on fluttering for nigh on eighty years. Dr Roberson was even the dentist in Dad's youth, before the pain was dulled by the needle, pulling the offending molars with ancient bone-handled instruments.

Outside work, shooting was the doctor's pride and joy, and he had won many cups for his prowess. One day, combining business with pleasure, he propped his gun in the corner of a farm worker patient's room, only to evoke the question: 'Ya baint come to shoot me, 'ave ya, doctor?' He also loved his garden, though he did not always see eye-to-eye with his gardener, Harry. Once, when potato planting time came around, he tried a new variety, constantly reminding Harry to plant them farther apart. This irritated the old man, until he finally retorted: 'Well, boss, they must be far enough apart, now; I've planted some of them in your garden, and some in mine.' But nobody was minded to answer him back when it came to matters of medicine, and he remained a Victorian in practice in a country village in the 1920s, with simple folk who trusted him.

So he laboured on through February, through the wheezes and sneezes and snuffles. But the month has so much more to offer than these human ailments – Candlemas bells, hazel catkins, arum lilies in the hedge bottom, primroses and rhubarb under tubs in the garden – surely the first fruit of the year, if fruit it be. February also brought some work that was always pleasing to me, for it is the best month of the year in which to layer a hawthorn hedge; at this time of year, the sap has started to rise sufficiently to allow the wood to bend without breaking, one of the considerations so important to the old-time farm worker. It is sad that the layering of hedges is becoming a lost art, like so much else; it really does give the hedge a good base, and if it is done well it is sheep-proof. As an added protection, the hedger would wrap the croppings from his layering around the chopped stools at ground level to prevent rabbits from eating the tender roots in spring. Today, I still admire the skill of the hedge layer as I see it from the car, but even the modern mechanical cutter trims hawthorn short back and sides, and what a tidy job it can sometimes do, reminding us of the neat railway hedges of years ago. It is unfortunate that the power-driven cutter beheads many hedgerow trees, but I have seen some farmers who sensibly leave the likely looking ash or oak intact when they trim a hawthorn hedge, determined to keep a firm control over the tool of their trade, rather than vice-versa. I am certainly not one of those old countrymen who regards the mechanical hedge cutter with contempt, the type who once

The proud men who played Cupid on Valentine's Day

forecast that cutting in this way would simply kill off our hedgerows; you have to speak as you find, and all I can say is that the hedges of the countryside are tidier today than they have ever been in my lifetime.

While we are making such comparisons in February, I must also add that today's printed Valentine cards are cheekier – and often simply downright filthier! – than they have ever been in my lifetime. But what a chequered career the Valentine has had, for although it came into use before the Christmas card, it had all but disappeared before its revival in fairly recent years. Early cards bore tender, sentimental rhymes, delicately ornate and lace-edged. Then came the crude and comic message of the anonymous sender – perhaps, in spirit, closer to the old pagan rite of drawing lots for women which was part of the original Candlemas celebrations, after the orgy of torchlight processions. Whatever is in his sack, however, no doubt the postman is still awaited eagerly on the morning of 14 February, as he was in this rhyme about an old country character:

> And on the morn of Valentine,
> His horn the village postman sounds.
> Then, halting 'neath the alehouse sign,
> Out many a blushing damsel bounds,
> Eager to seize the pledge of love,
> Painted with arrow, heart and dove.

CHAPTER THREE

March

Month of Many Weathers

Our ancestors christened this month March Many Weathers. It has sometimes been compared with a spoilt child, occasionally bursting out with laughter like sunshine and then, without the least warning, breaking forth into tears of rain or flouncing into a stormy rage. Nevertheless, March is a welcome month. The grass under the orchard trees starts to grow a little when the temperature rises to forty degrees, and the young lambs gambol when the evenings are lighter. It is a month of greening elder, of cuckoo-pints and violets. Shakespeare wrote of the sweet sound that breathes upon a bank of violets, stealing and giving odour. It is true that the scented violet blooms with little competition from other flowers. March is just one of the many months of the year when I think of Ralph, our old ploughman and carter. He whistled over the heavy field and he bore the burden of clay as it clung to his hobnail boots. Land ploughed by our four-horse team would often be left fallow, as it was too late for the sharp frosts of winter to break up the soil. The ploughed furrows stood up like long brown bacon rashers as a challenge to those pre-rotavator farmers.

Red Marvel wheat and Victory White oats were often sown in March on the clay, and we used a skim plough to make the tilth in which to sow the seeds. This implement, pulled by two horses, broke up a sugary mould two to three inches deep on top of the unyielding clay below, but it was a very different situation on the limestone hills. We had hill land on Bredon, and what a change it was from the Vale. There was no clay on our boots up there, but there were certainly stones to contend with. I once helped Ralph plant fifteen acres of Victory oats near Great Hill Barn up on Bredon. Two horses pulled a fifteen-furrow drill quite easily and the job went, as A.G. Street would have said, suently. We cross-drilled the field with sainfoin, our favourite clover. Working with Ralph high on the hill was like a holiday from the clay. We ate our 'bait' under the stone walls and watched the mad March hares boxing on the hillside. As we went to and fro across the field the only sound we made was the jingling of the harness and the snorting of the horses. After a few weeks the oats peeped through the stony land, pale green and tender. I was often sent up there to do what we called bird minding – scaring the pigeons and crows off the corn. Just imagine it, working as a human scarecrow! Days spent on the hill with a twelve-bore gun and black powder cartridges could hardly be called work. I sat under a wall waiting for the birds to settle on the young oats, and time went by slowly. The rabbits scurried about among the wild thyme in the parish quarry, and I would occasionally have a pot shot at them. But the does would either be in kindle or milky, and the bucks would be strong when cooked. No one really wanted rabbits in March . . .

As for those mad March hares, Ralph and I were not seeing things as we watched them boxing on the hill – though I can well accept that their antics have to be seen to be believed. Like the rabbit, the hare is nocturnal in its habits, coming out to feed at dusk and returning to its form, a tuft of coarse grass, at dawn. Unlike the rabbit, it never goes to ground – and in the spring when the bucks go courting they never go to bed, either, because they are active at all hours. They follow each other at a leisurely pace, occasionally interrupting the proceedings by fierce encounters. They chase each other around, jump high in the air while standing on their hind legs, and fight like sparring partners in the ring. The young leverets are born in early summer – to lead a life of monastic silence, except when they are in pain, perhaps after being shot or caught by a dog. Then their cry is like that of a child, sounding a little like 'ant, ant' to some people's ears. The country folk call rabbits not bunnies but bussocks – a strangely apt name, somehow, comical and undignified and affectionate, as indeed it is possible to feel towards rabbits if it is not your crop they are chomping through at the time. The hare, on the other hand, is Sally in country lore – a female name for what would seem a more gaunt and masculine-looking creature than the well-rounded rabbit. But then again, who was it who decreed that the daw should be the masculine Jack, or the pie the feminine Mag?

There was perhaps a certain rightness about wrens being Jenny, for there seemed something especially dainty and feminine about that tiny little weaver among hedgerows. But in the Vale there were so many other nicknames for birds, some no doubt shared with other regions, and others perhaps unique to us. Hedge sparrows were hedge Betties, yet another feminine name; woodpeckers were stock eagles, wood pigeons were quice, mistle thrushes were storm cocks, herons were mull herns, fieldfares were felts or velts, chaffinches were apple finches; even house sparrows were spodgers, as distinct from the 'spadgers' of many other corners of England.

Back in my role of a human scarecrow, I saw Shepherd Tidmarsh was working with his tegs in pens a couple of fields away, and I ate my bait with him in the shade of a wall. The field was stony and the feet of his hurdles were too long to drive into the earth among the stones. The shepherd lit his short clay pipe after we had eaten, and pointed to the twelve-inch-long feet on one of them. 'Old Charlie Moore makes them,' he said, 'and I've told him time and time again not to make the feet so long. The stone in this field is only just under the soil, and I

The rick yard shook to the rhythmic beat of the threshing machine

After long days in the field, there was much to be said for an afternoon's work in the big warm barn

Every countryman's dream: contented animals in the farm yard, with two prospering pigs as the centre of attention

can't get them in twelve inches. Tell yer Dad to have a word with Charlie. I'm sick to death of telling him about these hurdles.' Charlie, a mainstay of the village church bellringers, was a self-employed maker of hurdles and ladders. Hurdles were very much more a part of country life than they are today, though wattle hurdles made of hazel are still quite common, if only for garden fences; much more rare are withy hurdles, which were another of his specialities. Long, straight withies or willow poles were lopped from the brookside trees after seven years' growth, and after slicing off the small twigs, Charlie would split them, always starting at the narrower end. Using a cleaving hatchet, he hammered into the heart of the wood with a 'beetle', and the green withy would part in two half-round sections. Beetle is a Shakespearean word for a mallet, and the expression 'beetle-headed' refers to someone who is not very bright. The fromard was used to put into the split pole and then turned sideways, thus making the cleavage wider; and the cleft, as it opened, split the pole from top to bottom. This cleaving can be done only with the green withy, for the red, used for ladder rungs, does not have such a straight grain.

In his prime, Charlie could make a dozen hurdles a day. His curved draw-knife or draw-shave planed the green wood he needed for the rails or heads of his hurdles. These heads, like those of gates, were first of all drilled with a brace and bit. The holes were then joined up to form mortices with the help of a mortice knife, and tidied by the mortice chisel to receive the rails. Charlie, of course, had a wooden vice to hold his withy; but I also remember a device made from a horse's halter, operated by his foot, which held his work in place. No hurdle-maker used wire nails, but preferred a type that looked like small cart nails. These were clenched crossways over the grain of the wood to hold the cross-bracing to the rails, and the rails in the mortices. As for the feet, for all Alf Tidmarsh's grumbling, I doubt whether Charlie ever altered his pattern. Why should he? He had made hurdles all his life, creating folds for sheep using some tools that must have been known to medieval craftsmen at the very least. Little must he have realized, when starting out on his working life, that by the 1930s withy hurdles would be a thing of the past in his home county, superseded by wire netting and later electric fencing.

Even gypsy-made clothes pegs from withy wood are a rarity these days, the old pegs made by bronze-faced women sitting around their fire, splitting and peeling the sticks with a band of metal cut from an empty can until they were gleaming white. I miss those gypsies, their brightly painted caravans and their colourful washing drying on the hawthorn at their roadside camps. There were plenty of lean-looking dogs around those places, some so fleet that they could catch a hare. And though there was always a suspicion that the summer coats of their horses were shining like silk not only from feeding on the roadside grass but as the result of night-time grazing in other people's meadows, it was something that never worried me too much. I always had time for the dark-skinned Romanies, bonded by the closest of family ties, for ever in the open air and with such healthy children; and I shall never forget their nightly barbecues at sun-down in the coppices on the wide grass verges near the orchards; and yes, they played their violins, then, romantically and with passion, and sang ages-old songs in their traditional tongue.

On the farm, threshing was always a feature of our winter work, from harvest time right through until spring. It was always a good feeling to be doing the job by the time March came around, because it was a sign that your stores had seen you through the worst of the winter, and you knew that at this time of year the corn would fetch a good price at market, the autumn days of plenty being now a distant memory. But what a dusty job it was when I was a boy! A contraption known as the Winchcombe Tack – a steam engine pulling a threshing box or drum, with a straw tier pitched behind – drove into the rick yard on the afternoon before the work began. Joe from Greet was the driver, and he would shunt and shove the threshing drum alongside one of our ricks with his engine, and then couple the straw tier at the back of the machine. He then positioned his engine about twelve yards away from the drum, but in line, so that the long leather belt could be coupled from the flywheel to the drum's pulley wheel. Next morning he arrived on his bicycle at six o'clock to light the fire in the engine to get steam up for a seven o'clock start. Soon the steam began making sniffing noises from the valves, so that by the time the men arrived at seven Joe had already begun the whole orchestra of whirring pulleys and whining

Willows from the osier beds served a multitude of purposes in old-time country life

belts. In the early dawn the glare shone from the engine's fire box as he shovelled in more of the hard steam coal.

The flywheel turned slowly, the long leather belt purred, and every time a join passed over the flywheel the thongs of rawhide made a regular flopping sound. Chuff, chuff, chuff, the engine said as the men collected their forks and rakes, and it always seemed that the black monster with polished brasses was impatient to get going at full pace. The riddles went chunk, chunk, chunk, and the straw shakers clattered and danced up and down as an accompaniment to the low whine of the revolving drum. When Joe pushed the lever to full steam, the belt responded with a faster flap. The engine then sent sparks, smoke and steam through its chimney, and coughed louder and more often with its regular chuff, chuff, chuff. Tick, tick, tick the opening governors replied as their brass knobs revolved, and when Joe opened the whistle valve, the high-pitched blast made the farmyard fowl cluck and crow in anger.

As the farm boy cut the string on the sheaves, Joe stood on the drum beside the opening where the wheat-in-ear was coaxed inside by his sawn-off shuppick or fork. A pleasant fizzing could then be heard above the other, more strident, notes of the operation, as the grains of corn were parted from the chaff. The drum, now going at full speed, seemed to be answering: 'More, more, more. . .' If Joe failed to open a sheaf with his fork and it fell as a piece into the hidden depths of the drum, it answered with a wuff, wuff, wuff of anger, and showers of sparks rose from the engine's chimney. The monster behaved as if its heart had missed a beat, and it pushed its reserve power along the driving belt, which bucked and flapped between the pulleys. The corn made a constant 'shee-ee' noise as it fell into the sacks, while the chaff riddles went rack-a-tack-tack at full speed. The straw tier emitted a threatening sound before it threw out another bolting, almost like the audible warning given just before the striking of a grandfather clock. So the rough 'music' went on, hour after hour. Joe was occasionally relieved at his job of feeding the drum, and he would try in vain to silence the squeals of pulley wheels with oil squirted from his can. The singing of 'Drink To Me Only With Thine Eyes' by the boy who cut the strings round the sheaves blended, in a rustic sort of way, with the clackety-clack music of the machinery.

Then along came old Taffy, with his cap askew and his corded sleeved waistcoat, carrying two buckets of water suspended from a yoke over his broad shoulders. He had brought it from the pump to fill the half cider barrel where the engine sucked its life-blood for steam. The hosepipe in the barrel, when the water was low, added to the symphony by calling out chew, chew, chew. The men, amid clouds of dust, cupped their mouths and shouted above the threshing sounds into the ears of their workmates. And shout they had to, for the older men stuffed their ears with cotton wool to keep out the dust. A rat would sometimes run from the rick, chased by some of the inevitable band of little boys who would be watching the proceedings. It would squeal as a terrier grabbed it, and the lads would cheer as the dog tossed its prey in the air and yapped. At lunch time, Joe pushed the lever across to stop the engine. The feeder on the drum fed the loose-eared straw down into its mouth. The belt slowed the drum, pitched its note from tenor to bass and then stopped as the steam hissed from the safety valve. The men ate their bread and cheese on sacks of corn in the granary and slaked their thirst with cider. The raucous symphony was over for the time being.

Life was less noisy in March at the Hill Withy allotments, where the early Feltham gillies were blooming dark red and Frank was bunching the spring onions in the hut while Dick stood in Carrants Brook in his long waders washing more of them until they shone white-rooted in the sun. I always think of Hill Withy at this time of year, such a busy month for men devoted to their vegetable plots. Not that there was anything very special about this particular group of allotments, one of any number seized upon by ten-shillings-a-week land workers in the late nineteenth century as a place in which to grow more potatoes than their cottage gardens could produce, or to plant half an acre of wheat to help support the family. But it served its purpose, and now it is gone, and I believe it does not deserve to pass into complete oblivion without a few words to honour its memory.

When in the 1860s the Midland Railway Company ran a line from Barnt Green to Ashchurch known as the Loop, they released small parcels of land which were eagerly rented by the farm workers of the neighbouring villages. The one at Hill Withy, lying half way between the stations at Beckford and Ashton-under-Hill, served families from both those communities. It is true that there had been smallholdings before the railway, some of them created by the Enclosure Act of 1873; awkward-shaped pieces of land known as gores, they were considered too small and unattractive for the bigger farmers to work, but when the chance came to rent them at a few pence a year, there was never any shortage of takers. Not surprisingly, the railways created similar odd corners, and though the Ashchurch line is long gone, it is still interesting to travel other lines and look at the way the fields were carved in two when the line went through. In the case of the Loop, near the bridges where the embankments were thrown up for the old roads to cross, we can still see the boggy osier beds where the withies grew, slim, supple willow shoots so useful to the folk of the Evesham Vale for making fruit hampers and baskets. Hill Withy lay near Carrants Brook and the main road from Evesham to Cheltenham, and the railway let half a dozen one-acre plots on either side of the road where a decent-sized field had been carved in two.

Gypsy women whittled osiers and turned them into clothes pegs

Walter, a local publican, rented one of these plots in the 1920s. By then the practice of growing wheat and taking it to Sedgeberrow Mill to be ground for baking bread had long since ceased. Men did not reap and tie and stook the sheaves as their fathers had done. I remember Walter grew an acre of wheat on his plot and Ralph, our carter, cut it with the binder. When it was fit to carry, Walter enlisted the help of one or two of his customers to haul the sheaves with his horse and dray and build a miniature round rick on the old stone staddles in our rickyard. When our own farm ricks were threshed, Walter's was threshed, too. I do not know what he did with the corn, but I suppose his crop would have yielded about a ton of grain in those days. Another tenant of the railway company was Joe, a capable hedge-layer and a builder of stone walls on Bredon Hill. He grew potatoes and other vegetables, selling the surplus to the few retired gentlefolk of the village. On a weekly wage which was about £1 9s. 3d. by the 1920s, men with families were pushed to make a little money on the side. They either did long hours of overtime, bought fruit on the trees in the village gardens and sent the produce to market, or worked their allotments to grow vegetables and soft fruit to sell.

Along with Walter and Joe at Hill Withy were Dick, Bert, Tom, Jack and Frank. Frank, who had lost a leg in the First World War, was a remarkable man. I would say he did more work than most men with two legs; in fact there was no doubt about it. He could dig leaning on one crutch and he hoed in the same way, relying on his strong, muscular arms. He was also a great follower of the Croome hounds on Bredon Hill, and his giant strides as he propelled himself with his crutches made it hard for a boy like me to keep up with him. His sense of the direction in which the fox was going was equally remarkable, and the way in which he studied the wind and how the hounds would take the line of the fox from the wood on the lower slopes to the larches higher up would save those who walked with him a lot of climbing up and down the hill. On the acre he rented at Hill Withy he was in partnership with Dick, and together they spent long hours on the holding, growing strawberries, gillies, sprouts, peas, beans and some potatoes. There was no real road to the allotments, just a path across two fields, so Dick wheeled the produce of the land to Gypsy's Lane, where a carrier collected it for the market. By hard work, these men were able to make a little extra money in those days before income tax worried the working man. Jack bought himself a motor bike and was a cut above his fellows. He grew some lovely strawberries on Hill Withy and was the longest-surviving tenant, eventually retiring to Berkshire. He certainly survived the allotments themselves for many a year, but let us not forget the added dimension those plots brought to the fifty-two-hour-a-week men, that dash of independence as they tended their own precious land after tea or on Saturday afternoons. Beeching's axe saw off the Loop, and the last time I saw Hill Withy it was under barley, part of a larger field with the hedges, like the railway, swept away. A scene of change, then, but on bright March mornings you can still see the withy trees bursting their first tentative sprouts of green down beside Carrants Brook.

CHAPTER FOUR

April

Cuckoos and Cart Wheels

In Worcestershire, 20 April was always known as Cuckoo Day. It was the day of the Tenbury Fair, and it was said that you would never hear the first cuckoo of the year before then. But as the seasons vary, so does the coming and going of the cuckoo, for legend has it that before he went away from our shores, he would buy a horse at Pershore Fair and make for the coast. We have all heard his broken voice in early July, and the old folk used to say that this was when he did not get his horse at Pershore, waiting, instead, for the big fair at Stow-on-the-Wold. I do not doubt that there are regional variations of this tale up and down the country, but we surely all share that pretty little piece of lore that tells us that:

> The cuckoo comes in April,
> He sings his song in May,
> He changes his tune in the middle of June
> And then he flies away.

But the cuckoo apart, this is such a fine month for walking the wood-lands and watching the birds, before the trees are fully in leaf. The rooks have hatched their young and the incessant call of the fledglings, as the parent birds bring them their food, is just one of the pleasant sounds of an April day. High up in a lone clump of trees, the carrion crows call from their nests of twigs bound together like wattle hurdles – nests used time and time again, until they resemble little newly-thatched houses. The wood pigeon, or quice, as some country people call it, is a much less industrious bird, nesting in overgrown hedges and hawthorn bushes. Here the young are fed on what is known as pigeon's milk, regurgitated from the parent's beak. Starlings choose a hole in a tree to breed their young, before they nest in the very early spring. I never cease to be amazed at the sheer numbers in their flocks when they make their homeward flight to the woods at dusk. My favourite bird on the April scene, though, never enters the woods and coppices at all. Instead, the peewit or common plover nests on the undulating ground, laying maybe two or three eggs. This would seem to make its young vulnerable to a host of predators, and indeed they are. I always marvel at how peewits are so numerous, when hawks and carrion crows are so near at hand, ready for an easy capture.

The best time to walk in the woodland is, as the countryman calls it, 'the edge of night', or dusk. The rooks are still noisy but the quietness can almost be felt as the night draws on. When the trees have been swaying in the wind I have so often heard the eerie sound of limb rubbing against limb, like a creaky gate. The hen pheasants sit tight on their camouflaged nests among the brambles while a disturbed male bird

Cutting and loading timber could be some of the heaviest work on the land

might call 'cock up, cock up' as he flies to his chosen tree. Rabbits scamper to their burrows and thump the ground as a warning. The ashes are still bare but the oaks are showing new leaf, and under them the floor is a carpet of bluebells, their misty haze contrasting with the intense golden glow of the kingcups beside the stream. When he published *A Cotswold Village* at the end of the last century, J. Arthur Gibbs wrote: 'There is no more pleasing sound than the long chattering note of the woodpecker. It breaks so suddenly on the general silence of the woods, contrasting . . . in its loud, bell-like tones with the soft cooing of the doves and songs of other birds.' The local name for the woodpecker in Gibbs's day was the hick-wall or heckie, but in my younger days in the Vale of Evesham it was forever the stock eagle. Gibbs also described walking at 'the edge of night': 'It is sad to think that I alone of mortal men should be here to see this glorious panorama. It seems such a waste of nature's bounteous store, that night after night this wondrous spectacle should be solemnly displayed with no better gallery. The effects of light and shade which form part of English rural scenery are doomed to waste their sweetness on the desert air.' But the woodlands are not always so free of human activity, and I remember a job my father did as a youth, barking the fallen oaks in Dumbleton Wood. The bark was used for tanning leather in Evesham tanyard in the days before science changed this age-old method. Horses used in the timber team were knowledgeable animals, especially when the fellers called to them and the timber was eased on to the waggon with a roller chain. When a heavy tree was to be pulled, the carter often stood well back from his team and simply talked his horses through the task they knew they had to perform.

April has been called a fickle month, but that depends on what you expect of early spring in Britain. If April were to be bathed in sunshine without the showers, when the flowers are open-mouthed for rain, the blossoms would never delight us with that early spring freshness. I would prefer to describe the month as modest, rather than fickle. She is a maiden who is as faithful as flaunting May or passionate June, a green month with the tint of apple blossom and with violets and primroses blooming beneath the budding hawthorn and chestnut, those handsome candle-like chestnut flowers which never stay long enough with us. Our Saxon ancestors called April 'oster monat', or Easter month, and are said

Where would farm men have been without their carts?

to have held a feast in celebration of the goddess Eostre. It was Alfred the Great who decreed that the week after Easter should be kept holy. As for the hot cross bun, it was said to have medicinal properties in my grandfather's day. Several buns were hung over the chimney piece in the belief that they had a beneficial effect on the household; for instance, they could be grated, left for a full year and mixed with water to cure a child's stomach ache, and one of my uncles firmly believed in this reme-dy. Perhaps it was something to do with the penicillin in the mould! Good Friday has of course been a potato planting day for many years. I remember a neighbouring estate would give its farm men a holiday on condition that they would first go to church, but as congregations declined the custom died away. Another farmer allowed his workers to plant their potatoes on the headlands – 'addulands' – alongside the hedges of his ploughed fields, but he never let them work at all on Good Friday, preferring them to observe one of the popular rituals like trekking to the top of Bredon Hill; he would give them another day to plant their 'taters'.

I have a great love for April, and I remember that the cuckoo was always a favourite arrival in my boyhood days. 'Have you heard the cuckoo yet?' It was a question we asked each other on those mid-April mornings in the village. Really to appreciate the bird's voice, it has to be heard from afar, preferably over water. Some years ago I heard it one evening at Laugharne, from Dylan Thomas's old home, the Boat House, overlooking the Taf estuary. It called from the woods across the water as the tide lapped gently over the mud flats. The gulls were silent, and it had the whole stage to itself. Its call was all the more welcome since I stand by my view that the cuckoo is becoming an increasingly rare visitor. A well known naturalist publicly disagreed with me when I put forward this point of view a couple of decades ago, but I am certain that their numbers have declined because of insecticides, which rob them of their food. The creeping concrete of the motorways and the uprooting of hedges have also played their part in making this summer visitor feel

The timber of several native trees went into a cart wheel

A team of three takes the strain on the plough

unwelcome. As a boy, to hear four or five cuckoos in one field, calling from tree to tree from daybreak until dark, was company on the land before the noise of the tractor intruded upon the rural scene. Those were the days when the ploughman's whistle carried as clear as a bell on the frosty morning air.

But what has not diminished is the lore surrounding the cuckoo, a bird that lays her egg in the nest of some unsuspecting hedge sparrow so that someone else can do the incubating for her. Its arrival, so much commented upon and an annual topic of debate to this day in the letters column of *The Times*, has long been considered an omen. Gray in his *Shepherd's Week* describes the popular dread of hearing the first cuckoo in the spring, and the old custom of taking the shoe off the left foot when the call was heard. It used to be said that whatever you were doing when you heard that call, that would be your main occupation for the whole of the year. Young girls, on hearing it, would kiss their hand and hold it in the direction of the sound demanding: 'When shall I be married?' Old and infirm people would ask: 'When shall I be relieved from pain and affliction?' The cuckoo is perhaps the only bird called by the same name in all the European countries it visits, that distinctive call being interpreted in the same way everywhere. That is in stark contrast, for instance, with the rooster's 'cock-a-doodle-doo', which strikes the ear quite significantly differently from one country to another across the continent. As for the custom of calling late lambs cuckoo lambs, born after the arrival of that bird and the swallow, I do not know how widespread that is in Europe. But it was certainly common in my village when I was a boy, and I think of the little latecomers as that to this day.

I do not know about spring cleaning on the farm, but if the weather was beginning to look up at this time of year we would certainly be thinking of sprucing up our waggons for the summer. There was a majestic quality about those vehicles, often canary yellow in colour, that would stretch out like boats on four red wooden wheels with iron tyres. As far as I can tell, it was a close relation of carts brought over in the sixteenth century by Dutchmen employed to drain the Fens; but every county or district had its variation, from the spindle-sided Lincolnshire vehicle that still showed considerable Dutch influence to the hoop-raved

Time for 'bait': the true meaning of a ploughman's lunch

waggon common in the South Midlands. I think the hoop-raved type – almost unchanged, in my youth, from one portrayed by Constable in his famous painting of Salisbury Cathedral – was the most elegant of all; the raves were curled upwards above the hind wheels like the mudguards of an old car, and they had the bonus of adding to the carrying capacity. The old wheelwrights showed great skill in making their products, which were often 'dished', or concave with the hollow side facing outwards. One advantage of this shape was that it made the wheel stand out from the axle, allowing the waggon body to be made wider than that axle's length. It also gave strength to the wheels on uneven ground, avoiding the risk of their folding like an umbrella over rough land or on the side of a hill. Spokes were usually made of cleft ash; the wood had to be split or cleft with the grain because any cross-grain spokes would be liable to break. The felloes, or wooden wheel rims, were of elm seasoned before use, while oak was the chosen timber for the hubs, and beech for the axles. With ash again used for the shafts, and elm boards for the bed, the native woods of hill and vale were never put to better use. The year I was born, 1915, there were still more than 170 wheel-wrights in Worcestershire, which gives some indication of the amount of horse-drawn transport at that time, in a county with no major industrial city.

As we spruced up those carts, it was in the sure knowledge that as soon as they went out again spick-and-span an April shower would come along and spoil our best-laid plans. But they could teach you a lot for later life, those short, sharp bursts of rain, even if they did stop your work in the fields. I realized that one morning in 1931 when Ralph stood with me and Shepherd Tidmarsh at the granary door. 'It don't stop to rain,' Ralph said to the old man as the wind cut like a knife through the swaying walnut trees. I had been driving his four-horse plough the day before, but today we were all three of us kibbling slabs of cotton and linseed cake for the sheep.

'Oi, March don't finish until the twelfth of April,' the shepherd replied. ''Tis what they used to call the borrowing days when I was a bwoy afore the war.'

'Pop along to the stable, Fred, and give my osses another skip of fittle,' Ralph told me, and I carried a wicker hamper full of corn, mangels and chaff along to the great creatures, which all turned to me in restless anticipation when they heard my footsteps. Back in the granary, Ralph turned the cake-kibbler and the nuggets slid down into a bushel measure, ready for Alf Tidmarsh to shoot them into hundredweight sacks.

'Ast got a pipe o' bacca, Shepherd?' Ralph asked as he took his clay pipe from his waistcoat pocket. 'I ant had a whiff all day.' The shepherd chuckled and coughed, as he always did, and brought out his tobacco tin and his own pipe, which he kept tucked under one of the straps below the knees of his cord trousers.

'Must cut the lambs' tails,' he muttered quietly, watching the rain mixed now with sleet. 'But the wind's got to be in the right quarter, it's got to be downhill or south. Dost remember April 1917, Ralph, when the snow fetched the telegraph wire down?' And so they continued, these Worcestershire stalwarts of the furrow and the sheep pen, teaching the young strapper in breeches and puttees at their side more than they could ever have imagined.

Horses also enjoyed their version of the ploughman's lunch

The next day the weather cleared, and Ralph and I slushed our way up and down the furrows, ploughing in the same field where the shepherd's tegs or yearling sheep fed off the sprout stems. We had our ten o'clock lunch together in what they called the burra side of the hedge. Here tales were told of Ralph being hired out at the Evesham Mop to some hard farmer who fed him on cider sop – and at thirteen years of age he had no candle to light in his attic bedroom. Shepherd Tidmarsh, broad-shouldered and stout, boasted to Ralph that he had once ploughed with bullocks up Long Compton way, and produced some beetroot wine from his basket: 'Better than cold tay, any day.' There were memories of April Fool's Day, when the farmers used to send the boys on useless errands. They would fill a sack with stones and old iron and send the lad to the next farm with it, where the farmer would say no, it was not for him but for the next farmer along, and so on. Then Alf was back to his sheep and we returned to ploughing the sticky, wet clay, with Captain the filler horse at the rear of the team, then Big-Kneed Dick as lash horse, Boxer the body horse and big Turpin foremost. Those terms came as second nature to us in those days, body horse and lash, but how other-worldly they seem now. We were not very far from the home of Shakespeare, who wrote in *The Merchant Of Venice*: 'Oh Gobbo, thee has got more hair on thee chin than Dobbin the fill horse has got on his tail.' That is a sentence that would have sounded as natural as breathing on the lips of Ralph or Shepherd Tidmarsh.

CHAPTER FIVE

May

Splendour in the 'Gras'

May Day: it can mean a lot if you are a student of folklore, a socialist or a sailor in peril on the sea, but for our cowman Tom it was something else again – 'turning-out time', the day the cattle wintered in barn or yard were driven to the spring grass of the meadows. I remember as I helped him fodder the weaned calves in the barn and the yearlings in the yard he would often watch the winter wind and sleet sweeping in and mutter: 'Aye, it 'ull be a good job when May Day comes along.' Whatever the weather, that was when the cattle went out, unless it was a Sunday, and there was a kind of ritual about it all, in driving the calves from the built-up bedding of the barn, where the manure from months of winter reached half-way up the door. Never turn calves out on an empty belly or they will get blown eating the lush spring grass, Tom would say. 'Hoven' is the name of the condition when their stomachs become distended. So for the last time, the hay rack was filled at seven in the morning on May Day, and kibbled cotton and linseed cattle cake was put in the feeding troughs. By ten-thirty, when we had finished our mid-morning lunch in the warm barn, we had been joined by three more men or youths with bicycles.

As the door was opened, the three heifers stood with me in a circle around the inside of the outer yard while Tom tried to drive the young cattle from their winter quarters. First one and then another sniffed at the spring morning and then raced back into the semi-darkness of the barn. 'Give us a hand, Fred bwoy,' he called, and I took my nut stick and helped him persuade the first beast out into the open. Then another took the plunge, until all fifteen were at large in the yard. Tom and I knew nothing about blind ponies down the coal mines, but we saw with our own eyes the way the young cattle charged into the yard fences as the bright light blinded them for a short time. 'Let 'um run round for a bit and find their feet,' Tom told us, and with tails erect they sprinted and jumped in the air. We waited for twenty or more minutes until they were able to see where they were, and then Tom said: 'Let 'um go.' But go where? That was the problem. Young cattle that had never before seen the light of day or felt the hard road were difficult to drive.

We wanted to take them to a brookside meadow known as the Ham, which had been grazed by the April ewes and lambs so that it would not be too long and lush for these youngsters. The first four hundred yards, with some boys in front on bikes and Tom and me behind, went at a cracking pace, and the boys did a good job closing all the garden gates to make sure the beasts had only one way to go. But the last half-mile was completed at a walking pace, for it is surprising how quickly young cattle that have been confined to a barn get out of breath when they are first driven. In the end they were browsing the roadside verge of grass and vetches as we walked with our bikes to the meadow gate. Once in the field, the animals stayed close to the boundary fence, as if seeking the reassuring four-square presence of the barn around them again. Fear of venturing out into an open field is a very literal translation of agoraphobia, but it was a big surprise to see cattle suffering from such a complaint. Later, some feeding troughs and a bag of cattle cake arrived by horse and dray, and the calves recognized the sound of the kibbled cake on galvanized iron as I fed them. So for the second time that day they ate at the troughs – but not long after that, nothing would tempt them away from the spring grass. Tom and I walked together to the Ham after tea and found fifteen cattle chewing their cud as they lay comfortably full under the hedge. Early next morning I returned to the field, and it was with great relief that I saw that not one of them was blown. The precaution of turning them out to pasture with a foundation of hay inside them had proved wise. The thick winter coats of hair they had carried would soon become sleek in the summer sun, and by next winter these May Day debutantes would be strong enough to see the hard months through in the fields.

So not for us farm people the joys of tripping lightly round the may-pole on the first day of the month – and I recall that Jubilee Day in May

Little boys fishing in Maytime

1935, was not quite the holiday we expected it to be, either, for the weather was hot after a spell of good growing weather for asparagus. 'Gras', as we called it, was grown quite extensively in the Evesham area before the last war, mainly around Badsey and Bretforton but also on the clay land around Hinton-on-the-Green, with Newman's being the main growers. Next door, at Ashton-under-Hill, we grew about seven acres, but peas and sprouts always came first for us. The trouble with that Jubilee morning was that everyone had been given a day off to celebrate the Sailor King's twenty-five years on the throne – yet at the same time, the gras just had to be cut that day if it were not to be ruined, so about ten of us started out at first light. The buds stood soldier-like on the three-foot-wide beds, and I recall that that festive morning brought us our heaviest cut of the season.

By eleven-thirty the buds had been cut and were taken in pot hampers to what was known as the gras-house, where a group of women tied them into bundles with raffia. It was generally agreed that thirty buds went into each bundle, but as our asparagus was only moderate in size, the women made their bundles big enough to fill their boxes, and then placed the buds in such a way to make them look their best. Harry Bailey, Dad's partner, then took four bundles at a time, and with the help of a withy twig and a piece of webbing he held tight with his foot he made 'hundreds' of asparagus. He alone had this job of 'hundreding up', after which he would trim the butt ends of the asparagus with a sharp knife. Anyone could use the small sprigs from bundles of withies for 'dozening up' spring onions, but 'hundreding up' asparagus was a skilled job; and as for four bundles of thirty or so buds of asparagus making not 100 but 120, that was all part of the peculiar custom in the Vale of Evesham of using the 'long hundred' as a count for some of the produce of the land. It was a sort of baker's dozen; when the men planted cabbages by the thousand, it was usual to count out 1,200 plants. When plants were bought and sold for replanting, we counted out a similar quantity for each thousand. I never quite reconciled myself to the fact that men were expected to set out 1,200 plants with their planting 'pins' for only 1s. 10d., but that was life among the crops of the Evesham Vale in 1935. No doubt today our friends in the European Community would not agree with that method of counting, or with the baker's dozen; not that the modern baker goes along with that any more, anyway.

The relatively small quantity of asparagus produced today is packed in rounds, tidily secured with a piece of tape. The once familiar bundles of withy twigs are not seen nowadays outside agricultural suppliers in Evesham, for growers to tie up their asparagus and onions. Indeed, withies are no longer a crop on the banks of the Avon, or in the osier beds by the brooks. Pot hampers, ideal containers made from local withies, are now almost extinct, too, apart from in folk museums. These days, plastic boxes and nets from Hong Kong hold vegetables from the Vale more often than not. As for our Jubilee Day asparagus on that bright May morning in 1935, it was one o'clock in the afternoon before it was loaded on the dray by Harry Bailey and me and taken off to the local station to be sent on to Nottingham. I recall that it sold at half-a-crown a hundred, or 12^{1}/$_{2}$p if you believe such comparisons are meaningful. Today it is a luxury to be enjoyed by far fewer people than could afford it sixty years ago, but when my nephew recently grew parsley where the 'gras' once grew I was reminded that in my youth roast chicken with parsley stuffing would have been considered very grand fare indeed.

Happily, our long morning of cutting the 'gras' did not spoil the Silver Jubilee celebrations for us later in the day. The Jubilee committee had been meeting at Colonel Sykes's house regularly since the February, and as it was the first committee I had ever served on, I listened with interest to all the villagers' comments. Before the committee was formed, a general meeting had been held in the village school, and among matters discussed had been the menu for the festive meal. It was eventually agreed to have a knife-and-fork do of beef and salad and trifle in the chapel recreation room, but when it was found not to be big enough to seat all the adults, our earth-floored cart shed beneath the granary was swept out, whitewashed and furnished with a trestle table made from planks. The sports in the Little Wynch were quite an attraction, too, though all eyes at first were on the Big Wynch, where Fred Groves's Early Bird peas were standing blackened and devastated after the late frost. The sports, organized by Colonel Sykes, included not only egg-and-spoon and sack races and tugs-o'-war but a men's 100-yard handicap which was won by sixty-year-old Ralph Davies, with my father, at fifty-nine, second. Both ran in stockinged feet, and the fact that the third prize winner was Len Haines, an energetic young chap who prided himself as a runner, suggested that the handicapper was perhaps a little generous to the veterans. Other time-honoured events were a pillow fight on a horizontal pole between trestles, and a side-show where you sang for a pig, the winner being the one who got through the performance with the least giggles and the most control of the animal as you held it in your arms. When you consider the value of the prize in terms of the local economy, it was not surprising that many competitors kept very straight faces indeed.

It was a sweltering hot afternoon; the children had ice cream, and there was beer for the men – in moderation. The high tea in the cart shed turned out to be a real success, and the two women in charge and their team of girls kept busy bobbing back-and-forth from the recreation room with tea and heaped plates of meat. What I remember most

Cooling in barrels as the days grow longer and warmer

of all was a unique performance by a villager named Bernard Nicklin. He had a flair for making balloons out of paper, and with the aid of a methylated spirit light he would inflate them and they would take off. We all stood round and watched him at work. The air was still, and it was a splendid late spring evening. I can still see him as he lit the spirit beneath one particularly large paper balloon, and it came magically to life before ascending above the Little Wynch, higher and higher, before it disappeared over the Cotswolds. Soon darkness fell and we walked to the cuckoo pen up on Bredon Hill, where a bonfire had been built the previous Saturday. My father had made a kind of cave underneath the piles of hawthorn wood, with a framework of iron hurdles. This left room to creep under the wood with a bolting of straw, and light the fire from the centre. The heat was so intense that it partly melted the iron; there was speculation about how long the fire would burn, but as it turned out we were standing around a heap of red ash and the twisted hurdles in not much more than an hour. Nevertheless, as the rockets and fireworks streaked across the May night sky, we had a lofty vantage point from which to enjoy the celebrations of every other village in the Vale. It seemed that the whole skyline was ablaze with Jubilee bonfires.

Changed times, indeed – and that applies equally to the old boyhood pursuit of bird-nesting in May, long before mechanization and chemical farming resulted in the rarity of so many species that were commonplace when I was a lad. The English partridge is a good example, while the numbers of visiting cuckoos have also been reduced drastically by the toll of sprays and weedkillers on the insects on which they feed. It must be said, though, that even in my youth, we practised a Country Code years before that phrase had been coined. When we were bird-nesting we took one egg only from a nest, and once we had collected that species the nests were passed by. If the bird was sitting and the eggs were near hatching, nothing was ever disturbed. A lot can be learned about nature by walking along the hedges, through the fields and by the stream banks. If an egg was taken from a nest containing, say, four, if you went back the following day you would often find that the bird had laid another.

Our collections as schoolboys were kept in shoe boxes partly filled with sawdust, but when we were searching for an egg to add to the tally it was wise to be prepared. I carried a box lined with cotton wool in my pocket, and an ideal one was a container in which Dad's false teeth had come from the dentist. I suppose the skill of blowing eggs was learned from our elders. A small pin punctured the shell at either end, the yolk was carefully broken inside, and the contents were blown out with more or less difficulty. Large eggs like those of pheasants and moorhens were easy to blow. The small eggs of goldcrests and long-tailed tits, known as mummyruffians, were delicate and easily broken. The hours spent on Bredon Hill on the stony ploughland behind Grafton Firs searching for peewits' eggs are something I still remember. The parent bird would fly around us trying to deceive us by settling away from her nest, an example of the art of decoy well done. Partridges would feign injury and flutter along the ground with a drooping wing to attract attention away from their eggs. There always seemed to be so many house sparrows' nests in the thatch over the fowl house, with a variation of scribbles on their eggs. And I still like the look of starlings' eggs; we would find their

'Neath the spreading chestnut tree: the village blacksmith at work

nests in holes in the old cider apple trees and the eggs were plain, a beautiful green and a perfect shape. Not being much of a climber, I never ventured up to a rook's nest, but a friend of mine did once get an egg for me. I forget the total number of specimens in my collection, but I believe that they covered about forty species. Particular care had to be taken to get an owl's egg, since these birds are known to attack the eyes of an intruder.

Travelling to and from school in Evesham by train, I sometimes shared a carriage with a local ornithologist, F.C. Hiden, an interesting little man and a tailor by trade who visited local farmers measuring them for suits and breeches. He had a great collection of eggs, and in studying the habits and diets of birds, he proved that they did farms and crops more good than harm. When old turf is ploughed up, for instance, it contains a great many different creatures, especially leather-jackets and wireworms – and these are snapped up with gusto by rooks and other birds. I well remember one such field that was ploughed up and sown with runner beans. We all know that rooks will not eat run-ners, though they like broad beans, and when this crop was planted we were puzzled to see them scratching them out. In fact they were feeding on the wireworms that were feeding on the beans, clearing the field of the pest. One spring Mr Hiden wrote a letter to the *Evesham Journal* imploring farmers not to shoot rooks. His cry went unheeded then as it still does today, and I must confess that rook-shooting in May seemed good enough sport to me when cartridges were twopence each. I did it for years. Still, I often think of the old ornithologist's theory that in the bird kingdom, the good outweighs the bad. And I must confess that I was given food for thought after a shoot one May evening in more recent years, hearing the raucous calls of the parent birds as their fledg-lings lay dead on the ground. The nests had been riddled with shot, and all night long the adult birds cried out for their young.

CHAPTER SIX

June

The Umpire Who Wanted His Tea

June has always been a favourite month for country people. The fields are fresh, and the cool winds of May are forgotten in the sunshine. Autumn-grown wheat should come into blow – as Shakespeare would have said – in June. That was the Bard's word for blossom, and it is one that has always struck a chord with me. The ewes look clean and white after overnight rain, and the oats are growing well. There's an old saying:

> Oats in May make a man run away,
> Oats in June play a different tune.

It stems from the fact that the crop turns pale and sickly looking in the chill winds of May, only to bounce back into rude health in the June sunshine. Let's leave it at that, and not reflect too much on the fact that in recent years our Mays have often surpassed grey and soggy Junes for sunshine, just as Septembers have given Augusts a run for their money in terms of warm, dry weather.

Early one June morning in the late 1920s Ralph took two horses and a mowing machine to the plateau on Bredon Hill to cut the fifteen acres of sainfoin near Great Hill Barn. Sainfoin, or holy hay, loves the lime-stone hills and blooms with a red flower, one of the prettiest of clovers. I shall never forget its fragrance, either, and some of us boys even smoked the dried blossoms in clay pipes on Sunday afternoons! I had helped Ralph plant the ley the previous year, leading the foremost horse pulling a fifteen-furrow drill. This remote field of peewits and flat stones sur-rounded by stone walls was to provide the fodder for the lambing ewes the following spring. At ten o'clock I walked up the hill with Dad and found Ralph having his bait sitting on a corn sack under a wall. The swathes cut by the mower were already wilting in the sun, though the horses Boxer and Flower were helping themselves to an appetizing heap of it, and it seemed almost a shame to cut the proud red blooms in their prime.

'How's it going, Ralph?' said Dad, looking at the field.

'Pretty fair, Master, but the loose stones be a nuisance taking the edge off my knives.'

The carter cut himself a chunk of bread from the top of a loaf, and then he took a sliver of cheese. He was ready for his lunch. I had often seen him eating the top of a cottage loaf in this way, cutting it off deftly with his bone-handled knife, slicing the cheese to fit and eating his entire 'ploughman's lunch' off the knife. He would have had his breakfast at five, and then got his horses in and breakfasted them in the stable ready for turning out in the fields at seven o'clock. This ten o'clock lunch or 'dyow bit' – eaten when the dew was still on the ground – would be followed by dinner at three o'clock and tea at six. When the plough team was working some distance away from the stable, the ploughman would have lost time by eating at midday, so he kept going until nearly three, and then brought his horses back to the stables for their bait before going for his own dinner. After dinner he prepared food for them for the evening and groomed and watered them, while the plough boy cleaned out the stable. The older generation of market gardeners in the Vale of Evesham observed slightly different habits, tending to have their main dinner of the day at noon. It was only the toffs, of course, who had dinner in the evening, unlike today, but I do not see the current trend of dining at the end of a day's work as a sign that we are all acquiring airs and graces. With so many of us working a long way away from home, it is a rare family indeed these days that can conveniently gather together for a decent meal at the end of the morning.

'Have a swig of pop, Fred,' Ralph said, offering me a quart bottle with VAT 69 moulded on the side. 'It's some of thee Auntie Lucy's.' I knew what Auntie Lucy's pop was like; it was a staple drink in the hay and harvest fields of the 1920s. Accepting Ralph's offer, I was refreshed. Auntie Lucy made pop in the kitchen of her thatched cottage for most of the workers in the village. She made it from an ancient recipe from

All hands – and a few spectators – pause for the camera in the rick yard

the Black Country and sold it at 2*d.* a bottle, Camp Coffee bottles in the main. Although there was no deposit on her bottles, most folk in the village returned them to her, and if one was spotted empty under a hedge we would return it to her. Some haymakers drank cider, of course, but that was better left until knocking-off time! A clear head was needed on the waggons and ricks.

Some years ago Ewart Evans wrote a book called *Ask The Fellows Who Cut The Hay*, reflecting the fact that there has always been a mixture of art, mystery and fortune in haymaking. Grandad mowed the Avon meadows with a scythe; gangs of men cut the lush river acres by piecework, and he was one of that number who kept going from dawn until dusk. 'The art of mowing is whetting the scythe,' he would say. 'You must put a long edge on the blade with a whetstone, otherwise the scythe has to be sharpened more often.' They would put a young beginner in front of the team while the second man slid his blade close to the leader's heels, setting the pace. 'Keep the knowl down,' they would say, the knowl being the heel of the blade, near the sned or handle. It is history, now, the tales of these stalwarts who worked through the heat of the day and slept in the barns. If the farmer fed them well they would call: 'Ham and eggs, mind your legs.' If he was mean, the cry was: 'Bread and cheese, take your ease.'

The horse-drawn mowing machine changed everything, but in the 1920s I worked with men who had cut seven acres in the morning, when the dew soaked the swath. Ralph cut our hay with two horses abreast on his machine. When the sun shone hot and he changed his horses at dinner time I can still picture him sitting on the iron seat of his machine, the animals soon soaked with sweat which formed a white lather under their collars. Horse flies or 'old maids' were always a problem, stinging them on their chests and drawing blood. 'Whoa,' Ralph would call as they got irritated, and jumping from his seat he would walk round to the front of Boxer and Turpin, smacking them and killing the flies. He kept the pests away from their faces by hanging elder flowers from their mullins or blinkered bridles; they seemed to be especially badly afflicted in thundery weather.

Soon the sun changed the green swath into hay. The other men said it must have seemed like eternity to Ralph as he mowed the two hundred acres. It certainly did to Frank and me as we raked the swaths into wal-leys or windrows, with Flower and Pleasant pulling the rakes. It is true that we rode on the horse-rake – but what a ride, on an iron seat over hard ground. When the men came with the waggons to pitch the load one day, the shepherd said: 'It's never fit. It wants another day's sun and it'll get hot.' Tom, our cowman, always swore that a farmer who never made a hot rick never made good hay. If the hay was over-made George said it was slick, and as he pitched from walley to the waggon, my Uncle Jack had a job keeping the corners of the load square. It was so much easier ricking the hay in the field. It saved a boy like me steering two horses and a waggon through the ten-foot gateways and up the road into the rickyard. Before I was allowed to ride a horse-rake I led the horses in the field, feeding them with hay as they stood, until George called 'Hold tight' and Uncle Jack steadied himself with his shuppick or pitchfork as the half-loaded waggon moved on.

As a boy I loved listening to the chat in the field and rick yard. When a forkful of hay was suddenly taken up into the sky by a whirlwind the men looked glum. 'Tempest,' said Tom.

'No,' the shepherd would retort. 'Not until the sun gets down along with the wind.'

And so it would go on until little Uncle Jack would shout: 'Let's have it, you chaps. Have it up in a yup.' The pitchers worked in shirt sleeves, with battered hats to protect them from the sun and to keep some of the hay seeds from them when they crawled under the waggon raves to rope the load. If the rain came, turning the hay a blackish grey, some said it was fit only for litter, but Tom would sniff a bit under his nose and say:

'Ah, it unt the best o' fodder, a bit mouldy it'll be for the cattle, but I'll tell you summat, Fred. The cattle would sooner ut this than their fore feet or a snowball when winter comes.'

Harry Bailey was with us in the field. He raked up every bit of hay, telling us that we should never waste any as the cattle would need every mouthful. He was right, of course. At the rick another small gang worked, unloading the waggons. The shepherd built the rick and a tidy job he made of it, despite the fact that he had said that it wanted another day's sun on the hay. When a handful of green grass landed from the unloader's shuppick he would carry it to the outside

The knife-grinder was always a welcome visitor in an age when chores both at home and at work relied heavily on hand-held tools

Winter meant hard times, and not all countrymen could allow themselves the luxury of admiring the sight of snow on thatch

Paintings 1, 2, 3, 4, 7, 8: Fine Art Photographic Library Ltd; 5, 6: The Bridgeman Art Library.

of the rick, muttering: 'That's what 'ull make it fire if that goes in the middle.' The rick grew higher until Dad and Jack, Bert, Fred and Uncle George put up the elevating pole. Dad got the men to lay the pole on the back of half a load of hay. Ralph or Jack would back the waggon until the pole was nearly upright, and a man at each of the guy ropes pulled, on instructions from Dad, until the pole was upright and the guy ropes were pegged down. The jig, a crane-like device, swung with dangling forks from the waggon to the rick, and each time the horse on the rope that lifted the forks was led forward, a great load of hay was swung on to the rick. A quick way of unloading, this, and of building a high rick.

When night came I remember Jack or George hooking a trace horse to the waggon's back axle while another man held and guided the shafts. And so the waggons were drawn away from the rick, empty and ready for the following day's loading. Now came the job of getting old Alf Tidmarsh, the shepherd, down the ladder from the roof of the rick. One man held him while another steadied the trembling ladder, and the old man slowly descended. He wiped his damp brow, gazed from the ground up the stack he had erected, and said: 'Not for five pounds would I go up that ladder again.' In this way I saw men work hard and lose sweat for the animals' winter feed. Here was humour – and here was panic, too, when George looked up at the rain clouds and declared: 'It looks black over Bill's mother's.' And most of all I remember the horses when I took them to drink long and deep at the pool at the end of their long, dry day in the field, and the collars falling on their necks as they lowered their heads.

I also remember our hens in summer, when the ricks were new and the nettles were high beside them. Every year a number of our white Leghorns would lay astray among them and then go broody and sit there for three weeks, easy prey for a night-prowling fox. We always thought we were lucky when the wanderers would eventually reappear, proudly strutting towards the yard gate with a lovely little batch of custard-coloured chicks. I think you could safely describe those birds, and indeed the ones we kept that observed more conventional laying habits, as free-range. They would scratch around those staddled ricks, peck at mangolds and oat flour and blackberries and windfall apples, and enjoy

There was never much rest on the Sabbath for the railway track crews

on top of that an official diet of wheat and maize, half and half. I shall never forget the way they descended from all points of the compass when the farmer's wife called 'Biddy, Biddy, Biddy' and broadcast the corn in the yard. In winter they were given a hot mash made mainly from boiled potatoes, and I believe they enjoy hot food in topcoat weather as much as we do. No one bought grit for hens in those days. The birds helped themselves from the almost empty roads, and they found worms in the muck heaps. It is true that they could look a scruffy lot, sometimes, bedraggled on wet days when they sheltered under bushes. They would come home to roost with their plumage soiled and the eggs in the manger in need of a wash – but I shall always prefer the golden yolks of the insect-eating scratching bird to the products of the modern battery hen.

And what an adventure it was collecting the eggs from those 'barn door' birds. Some laid in orange boxes lined with hay in the fowl house, while the ones that perched all night on the laths of the hay loader in the barn were up at dawn and laid in the cow manger or somewhere else. All this meant that collecting was a round of surprises. The fierce old broody hens often covered the eggs laid on the ground under the manger. It was quiet there, but it was tricky to get the warm eggs without a few sharp pecks on the back of the hand. We often had to pick the broodies, squawking and protesting, from the nest, and learned once more that they were fearless mothers. I know that if a rat from the barn became interested in a stray chick, the hen would attack with outstretched wings until her brood was safely under her feathers.

Our ducks were quite a different case. They were not allowed out of their thatched pen until about ten o'clock in the morning, for by then they had laid their eggs on the earth floor instead of by their pond. Wonderful layers, the ducks were, but what a game it was getting them home off the ponds and brooks in the twilight of a summer's night.

My final memory of haymaking was the scene in a Sunday morning rick yard, with as many as nine or ten loaded waggons waiting in line to be transformed into new ricks on Monday morning. All vehicles were loaded on Saturday so that the hay would be safe from any Sunday storms – and it is all a reminder of how much the observance of the Sabbath has changed in my lifetime. In my childhood there was an almost Victorian feel to it. Families walked to church or chapel in their best clothes, the men in black, with bowlers or trilbies for those with aspirations and caps for the rest. My turn-out as a child consisted of a black coat, pin-striped trousers and an uncomfortable stiff collar. No work was done on the land, except the feeding of cattle and lambing of ewes. The cart horses would be given bran mash on Saturday night to clear out their system, and the next day they rested contentedly in Boss Close, the home ground, rolling on their backs and showing shiny, hard-worked shoes as they did so. After church the farm men strolled from one garden to another, comparing the early potatoes and the pig in the sty, and drinking a tot of cider as they did so. No hoops or tops were bowled or spun in a Sunday village street, but if the weather was fine the afternoon brought the whole village out for a walk across the footpaths or up the traffic-free roads; even cycling was seen to be not quite acceptable on this day devoted to rest and worship.

The walk along the snaky single-track lane to Kersoe, with grass growing up the middle, was a favourite; it was a dusty track in summer, while the soaked gravel earth and chippings clung to our boots in wet times. Men normally employed in plough or field work walked briskly with their families in cotton-laced light boots known as tea-drinkers. What a relief it must have been to be free from the heavy hobnailed boots of the working week. At six or six-thirty, these same folk would walk with squeaky boots up the church or chapel aisle, to listen to our preacher Emanuel Jones and perhaps perform some simple duty or other. Some would pass the collection bag. One, I recall, gave a loud puff to blow out the altar candles. Whether or not they as individuals were more devout than those who make up today's dwindled congregations is a matter for conjecture. Let us remember that the religious houses of those days were a centre, too, for the social life of the village — the teas, the fêtes and the Sick and Dividend Club were a part of church life. I even remember one man in our village who had what was termed 'the audacity' to declare himself an atheist.

We were warned constantly at chapel of the threat to the British Sunday and the coming of what was known as the Continental version; I had a vision of all that was evil and unwholesome taking place across the narrow sea at Calais. Of course, there was already some precedence for Sunday activity locally. The four platelayers in the village employed by the Midland Railway were well used to being called out to mend the track on the day of the week when traffic was light, and by the late 1920s four-shilling half-day trips to Weston-super-Mare were available from our station. But even then, few people read a Sunday paper and children were allowed to read only religious material or stories with a moral. It was the Second World War that changed everything. Suddenly, farm machinery could not be left idle on Sundays, and harvesting was at least as important as making bombs or shells in Birmingham. The so-called Continental Sunday was all but with us, and there was no turning back from it.

But that was all in the future in the 1920s, when at midnight on Sundays in June it was once again back to the land, with the men sitting on pot hampers waiting for the clock to strike. Then they would grope in the moonlight for strawberries for Monday's market. Yes, it has been the same for ages in June: haymaking, strawberry picking and cricket. The women in their bonnets picked strawberries as soon as it was daylight, ready for the early morning market. Before and after Sunday school I would be banging away at the starlings with a number three garden gun, keeping them off the ripe fruit. Sunday school was now practising, sometimes in the vestry, for the July Anniversary, the little annual eisteddfod at the chapel. There was verse, song and recitation among the flowers on the platform. My friend Frank recited: 'A lawyer I will be, because it pays those who interpret laws,' while I followed with:

'And I will be a railway guard, and blow my whistle shrill and hard.'

On Saturday afternoons there was cricket in the meadow beside Carrants Brook where Fred Tandy had prepared a perfect wicket. The turf was like the green of a decent golf course, thanks to his loving care, but that description did not quite apply one Saturday when he fell ill and a friend of mine called Jim who mowed the pitch omitted to put on Tommy the horse's leather shoes. Hoof marks on the wicket forced us to play the fixture away, and it was rare that we travelled to a ground as good as our own. I have played on some pitches where only the square near the wicket has been mowed reasonably short, with the outfield grazed by cows driven away just minutes before play began. You could easily lose the ball in the lush grass around the boundary – and white flannels and cow pats were not always too compatible.

Sometimes the men would leave their work in the hayfields and make for the match. Cricket was a religion like church and chapel. A navy and yellow flag hung from the pavilion, where the two sides had their changing rooms labelled Home Team and Visitors. It was a true pavilion, a far cry from the old railway van that served the purpose years before, as well as acting as a notice board at election times, bedecked by yellow or blue posters for the rival candidates. This new building was a gift from Sir James Curtis, who was knighted for his good work in the Food Ministry during the First World War, and he and the few gentlemen of the village sat in a privileged place to encourage the players as they came down the steps to face the bowlers at the crease. I remember the incense-like cigar smoke and the reverent clapping of these grey-moustached, well fed, gold watch-chained members of the club. Whitsun was usually in June, and on fine Whit Mondays we played Alcester and Ragley all day. This was one of the days those gentlemen truly came into their own, providing us with a free salad lunch; or at least they provided the money, for it need hardly be said that the food itself, as always, was set before us as a result of the labours of a band of mothers, wives and girlfriends.

The cricket club was founded in 1907, rule seven being: 'The committee reserves the right to dismiss any member for disorderly conduct on the field.' In the August of that season the owner of the club's first field, a farmer named Frank, gave notice to the club that he refused to let Arthur, a neighbouring farmer, play in any match that season because of some grievance between them; the fact was that Arthur had let his cattle stray on to Frank's mowing grass. The committee met, with the curate in the chair, and decided that Arthur had broken rule seven. Arthur, a doughty character who always claimed he had once bowled out W.G. Grace, was not going to be daunted by petty officialdom of this nature, and the next season he was fielding a team of his own, the United Club, which a couple of years later came back into the fold of the village team.

The beauty of village cricket is the varied make-up of the team: men who had learned to play correctly at public schools, farm labourers whose agricultural strokes often surprised the best bowlers when a good length ball was put away for six over the withy trees and, in our case, Archie Butler, the village blacksmith, who used his bat like a sledge-hammer. He came from the Forest of Dean, and allegedly answered an advertisement in the *Evesham Journal* for 'A blacksmith, preferably one who can play cricket.' He did not wear cream flannels, but silver-grey ones, with broad braces and a thick leather belt with a brass buckle. A flat pancake cap and tattoos on arms like legs of mutton completed the effect – but you did not hear opposing teams sniggering about him for long. A good ball on the off side was sometimes swept to the square leg boundary. The better the ball, the more effective were Archie's strokes. After making sixty runs one Saturday he said that was the last time he'd do it, since they had drunk all the cider in the pavilion during his absence at the wicket. But he surprised even himself with his all-time biggest hit, which ended up in Gloucester, twenty miles away. It had landed in the truck of a passing goods train!

The umpire was always a scapegoat if things went wrong, and I still admire the pluck of those men. Charlie, our hurdle-maker umpire, was once asked 'How's that?' to which he replied: 'Not out, but if it occurs

Local cricket teams brought all ranks of men together to fight a common cause

again it will be.' But he was no respecter of persons, as he proved one Saturday when Ewart, who had won his county cap, turned out for the village and took leg stump as his guard when he arrived at the crease first wicket down. His first ball was well wide on the leg side, and he padded it away in true county style. 'Out!' roared Charlie. 'LBW!' Our cowman told me later that as he stormed up the pavilion steps, Ewart used a word 'that unt in the Bible nor the prayer book – but cricket is after all a game, and games can go on too long.' On another occasion the last two batsmen were making a lot of runs for a neighbouring team and our bowlers just could not separate them. There certainly did not seem to be any grounds for an LBW appeal when the ball struck one of the tail-ender's bat and pad together, but before we knew it Charlie was up on his toes with his finger in the air bellowing 'Out!'

Our captain said: 'He can't be out. He played the ball with his bat.' But Charlie, gazing straight down the line of the wicket, would have none of it.

'The ball hit him on the leg,' he growled. 'He's out; and any road, I wants my tay.'

An umpire who followed Charlie was Harold, a retired insurance manager, who would sit on a shooting stick and was devoted to Rex, his fox terrier. Our captain at that time was a cricket devotee who would often leave the hayfield to play. He was also a man with a great sense of humour, although it was one not always appreciated by visiting teams – especially when he had ducks painted on the tin number plates that were hooked on the score board, instead of the usual noughts. No one likes to be out for a duck, and that white Aylesbury on a black background really did seem to be rubbing it in. One Saturday in early May, when the wicket was still soft and the ball rarely reached the boundary fence, the village boys were getting bored. Harold's beloved Rex was watching his master at work from beside the score board, and some of the older lads hit upon the bright idea of catching him and tying one of the metal ducks to his collar. The terrier trotted around the boundary fence quite unruffled until Harold spotted him from the middle. Putting aside all thoughts of his duties as umpire, he charged towards the group of boys, threatening them with his shooting stick. That was how unpredictable cricket was on our green and pleasant field.

So June passed apace until the 26th, Pershore Fair day. It was a horse fair in those days, but it had roundabouts and swings as well, even though the ox and pig roasts were long gone. It was good to see Pershore alive for that one day of the year, however, good to feel the sense of occasion as the great shire horses converged from the surrounding villages with their manes and tails 'done up' neatly with straw and ribbons of red, white and blue. For the Evesham asparagus growers, it was time to put away their pronged knives for another year, for buds that remained after Pershore Fair were best left on the plant to grow into bower. And there was sadness, too, a mark of time passing, when the cuckoo bought his horse at the fair and galloped off to warmer climes, not even waiting for the full warmth of an English high summer. Only the braver birds stayed on into July to select their steeds at Stow.

CHAPTER SEVEN

July

Fields of Primrose Ewes

July is usually the hottest month of the year, when the land is warm after the longest days of late June. But it is often a wet month, too, and it can be a trying time for the animals in the field, with cattle tormented by the bree fly and sheep by bluebottles. Looking back over the years, I remember how glad we were that the ewes had been shorn in June and that their heavy fleeces were no longer a harbour for the flies to lay eggs in the damp, warm wool. Still, the flies turned to the lambs, and struck at the soiled part of the breech, soiled because of the flush of grass that had scoured the stomachs of the four-month-old animals. The cure for that was a minute per lamb in the dipping bath, where an arsenic mixture blended with yellow ochre gave protection from fly blows for a month or so. When compulsory dipping took place, notice had to be given to the village policeman, who timed each sheep as it passed through the bath. The constable would stand, in full uniform, by the sheep wash, and call out 'Right!' when the sixty seconds were up. Then the shepherd used his crook to guide the animal through the bath and give it one last total immersion for a second or so. He then stood back as the bedraggled, indignant looking and yellow-tinged sheep clambered the ramp to the draining area; this was a hurdled passage with a corrugated iron floor laid so that surplus chemical ran from the sheep back into the bath. The practice of adding yellow ochre to the bath has been discontinued now, as the wool merchants do not care for coloured fleeces. One reason why breeding ewes went round a primrose yellow in those days was that it was said that it made them look bigger for the market. I admit that they did look rather attractive at the Kerry and Clun sales I used to attend at Craven Arms.

In our village our numbers were increased in July by the arrival of the pea pickers. About a hundred of them camped out with sacking bivouacs under the hawthorn hedges or slept in the straw in the barns or cattle sheds, and a kind of multi-racial society sprang up in the pubs and shops. It worked well enough. Their names were the same as the places they came from, Stafford, Scottie, and yes, one man even went under the name of Manchester. What a fascinating past these wandering folk would recall – and so often their theme was the same, harking back to the blight of the First World War, which had wrecked a settled life forever. Some came from the less salubrious parts of Cheltenham, bringing their families for a summer holiday in the country away from the cramped town, where they spent the rest of the year selling fruit and flowers from barrows. These people, a close-knit community, copied on a lesser scale the Black Country folk's emigration to the hop fields of Herefordshire, or the more famous working holidays of the East End cockneys in Kent. I suppose the ones who interested me most of all were the travellers, wayfaring men who came as regularly as the black-winged swallows. I saw the same faces each year claiming the same stalls in the sheep barn, where rough-hewn boards partitioned the long thatched building. These footsore tramps would bed down here in the pens where the ewes had lambed in March, and though some of them had a woebegone look after a hard winter, they proudly showed their war medals and faded ribbons on their threadbare jackets.

The one they called Scottie was an upright man, tall with a waxed moustache, who swaggered as he walked from the turnpike to the village cross. All his worldly goods were packed in a sack which he carried on his back – all, that is, but an enamel mug and billy can which hung from a leather belt around his waist. Darkie came with him, short and swarthy and a little bent after years spent as a navvy. These two were early risers who picked the pea pods from the haulms as the first light of morning was shining over the dew-drenched fields. Darkie worked faster than Scottie, an ex-ship's engineer, and it was easy to see why. Scottie was an educated, eloquent man who would have equalled many a Hyde Park orator as he expounded on religion and politics to the motley crowd who sat on wicker pot hampers picking forty pounds of peas for a shilling. In the evening he would sit on a log smoking his clay pipe and waiting for his dinner, stirring mustard in an old egg cup as

The village constable keeps check on his watch as sheep take their statutory minute's dip

Darkie stoked the fire. Here tales were told of the ocean liner that had carried him around the world until gambling became his ruin. On Sunday he would walk up our village street like the squire, smoking his pipe and resplendent in a new cap and clean corduroys and carrying a forked nut stick. Sacco and his sandy-haired wife stayed with their brood of children at the other end of the barn. She came with a pram loaded with life's bare necessities, and knew well how to make herself useful. She could use a scythe, and often cut down the stinging nettles in the orchard when there was no pea picking to be done. Annie Shaw slept in a stable manger and Tich in a waggon in the cart shed which he shared with a heavily whiskered old character known as the Man with the Dog. He would pare his corns with an open razor, and I still shudder at the thought of that! The man called Manchester was an ex-serviceman and a great pal of one Joe the Doings, and they both slept out in the pea fields by themselves under a bivouac of sacking.

The early morning in the pea fields was heralded by songs, chatter, the smell of twist tobacco or the wood smoke from a fire boiling tea. The billy can, made from a big cocoa tin with a wire handle suspended from a length of iron rod, was continually brewing tea until nightfall. And in the evening, I often stood until late under the peasgood nonsuch tree at the back of the barn, where another wood fire burned between smoke-stained bricks. There, potatoes and the inevitable peas would boil in a Bluebird toffee tin, the lid of which was used as a frying pan for corned beef bubbling in margarine. It is strange how everyone got on together, and the singing on the benches outside the Star Inn was loud and long after the travellers had sought to ease their aching backs with cider after cashing in their tin tallies for a shilling each at our back door on a Friday night. These discs, marked 'HB Henry Bailey' – the name of my father's partner – were issued by Uncle George in the field, one for every forty-pound pot filled. They could not have dealt with a more fair-minded man than my uncle, a lifelong teetotaller and plain-dealing workaholic who sometimes found some of our more colourful casual workers a little hard to take. One year a gypsy family arrived, five of them; then came their relatives, also claiming work. 'I'm their cousin,' said one. 'I'm their auntie,' said another. It all became very tangled and complicated, and entirely beyond poor Uncle George.

Pea picking also attracted the village women – or at least, the prospect of a few extra shillings did – and they came early to work carrying their peck baskets or buckets, still wearing the herden aprons and cotton bonnets that made the pea field such a picture on sunny days. The bags and hampers of peas were loaded at our little railway station for the town and city markets of the North, and all day long the dray horse Flower drew the loads to the waiting trucks. These were the days when there was a season for peas, before they were eaten all the year round from tins and freezers. I well remember the first tin of peas we ever had, and Dad pouring away the green liquid, swearing it was vitriol! A far better memory was our cooking of the first peas of the new season – and looking forward to the return of Scottie, Darkie and the rest.

By now the villagers were digging young potatoes in their gardens and allotments, and were generally dining better than they had been at the beginning of the year. Spring peas, broad beans, young potatoes and boiled bacon were a typical dinner for the men who worked the land and were up early in the morning for their ninepence-an-hour overtime. With bent backs, groups of villagers moved to and fro through the endless rows of Brussels sprouts, hoeing around the growing plants. They were quiet compared with the pea pickers, for the only sound was that of a file sharpening the hoe plates when the workers reached the edge of the field.

At our village chapel the Sunday school scholars had performed at the traditional July Anniversary, and raised enough money for the annual outing to Weston-super-Mare. And what a day that was. At six-thirty on a Saturday morning a steady stream of children, parents, youths and girls made their way towards our little station. There was a race by some of us to jump on the weighing machine in the waiting room and compare statistics, and on limited pocket money it was still difficult to overcome the temptation to drop a penny piece through the slot for a slim bar of Nestlé's chocolate. The train left at seven o'clock, and what a motley crew we were heading for the delights of the Bristol Channel: men in dark Sunday suits and trilby hats or flat pancake caps, ladies in their Sunday finery. Some of the children carried buckets and spades for the beach. As a boy of fourteen I was allowed free range for the day with my friends Geoff and Frank. When we arrived at Weston we took the tram to Birnbeck, the Old Pier, a vehicle bearing the proud and true legend: 'The Tide's Always In At The Old Pier.'

Our four shillings were spent on a trip on the steamer *Ravenswood* to Cardiff, but we had to be back in England by five o'clock to help with the singing of 'Be Present At Our Table, Lord' before our high tea at Brown's Café. Those outings to Weston are remembered as fine and sunny days – but it did rain, of course, when St Swithin shed his tears and christened the apples.

Another time we took the train to Malvern, and climbing to St Anne's Well soon after we had arrived, we drank from the Crystal Spring and our

Freedom calls: the flock heads back to the field after dipping

young minds were touched by the figure of blind George, one of our number, who played on his portable harmonium. 'A lesson, here,' said Mr Cotton, our superintendent. 'How precious is our sight.' And we stood at the summit and looked with awe at the view, with Wales – another country – in the distance. Closer to us was the pastured plain stretching towards Ledbury, and there were few who felt inclined to disagree when the teachers emphasized the words written on a plinth near by: 'The earth is the Lord's and the fullness thereof.' We played rounders on a flat patch of wiry grass and slid down the slopes before it was time for tea – this time at the Dorothy Café. Our tables were booked, and other customers paused when one of our teachers gave us the note for singing grace. Our eyes should have been closed, but the sight of raspberry jelly, blancmange and trifle was too much for our concentration. It would be back to bread pudding for some of us on the following day.

James Cotton, in his bowler hat and white starched shirt front, was typical of many of the good people of the 1920s who devoted their spare time to the religious and moral upbringing of their neighbours' children. He himself had little schooling as a boy, but he amassed a great knowledge of the land around Bredon Hill and the people who lived on it, and as our superintendent he was a teacher in more ways than one. He especially liked to retell Old Testament stories, relating them to his own experiences. His personal story was that of a boy of eleven who left school to drive the bullocks at plough up on the hill. As a shepherd later in life, he found work with Arthur Roberts at the village's Old Manor Farm, working his way up to what would now be called a farm manager. He had a sound eye for animals and an instinct that told him whether stock was thriving or, to use a local expression, 'looking unkind'. When I first knew him he was head gardener of a house in the village, The Close, where he took special pride in the roses and daffodils. I also remember him playing the big brass viol in chapel, and singing in a bass voice as low as Paul Robeson's. Recitations at village concerts were another party piece, and when he played the bones in time to the music, it struck me that the big beef bones he chose were somehow an appropriate equivalent to his low singing voice. At parish meetings he was a mine of information on subjects like footpaths, rights of way, drains and water courses, and it came as no surprise to us, years later, when his services as a water diviner were suddenly indemand. He used not the traditional hazel twig but a home-made

Travelling labourers and their families relax after a long day in the fields

contraption around his wrist, integral parts of which included various copper wires and the gold knob off an umbrella. The knob rotated when he stood over an underground spring of water, and he would then follow the hidden stream to its source. Some wells still to be found in the Vale of Evesham today were dug where James Cotton had divined water.

He went through life noticing the passing scene, making mental notes of the ways of wild birds and the weather. Like his contemporary, the poet W.H. Davies, another self-taught man, he found time to stand and stare. But he was a doer, too, to the extent that there were times when I wondered what he could not do. He was a keeper of bees, making straw hives known as skeps, and I can still picture him with a veil over his straw hat taking the swarms in June. Blue Persian cats were another of his passions, and I remember how he proved how harmless grass snakes were to man by nursing one under his shirt. He had few equals as a hedge-layer, and when he grafted Pitmaston pears on to hawthorn stock he produced trees that fruited abundantly for fifty years or more. And I must not forget his ability with a scythe, for the lawns of The Close were as well tended as if he had used a razor. I worked with him one wheat harvest when he built our ricks, and they were as solid as the cottage he lived in. I often look back and wish I had looked more closely into this unusually versatile man's philosophy in life. He allowed himself a little self-satisfaction when he reflected that 'I have never rubbed my back against a college wall,' but his was a truly gentle and humble nature; and out on those Sunday school outings, as at all other times, he was truly a man whose company was a pleasure.

The irony was that our own village of Ashton-under-Hill was the destination of many a Sunday school day out for town children from Evesham, and I recall the crocodile of pupils and teachers carrying bats, balls, hampers of sandwiches and cakes and other good things stretching almost the length of Station Road when they arrived. The boys and girls played cricket and rounders in the church close, among the shady oaks where the grass was short on the footpaths. Of course they were scarcely urban children, coming from a small country town like Evesham. But a lot of them were very poor, and they revelled in the freedom of simply being away from their familiar streets; broody hens were understandably angry when little boys lifted them off their nests in the cow shed, and the rick yards were ideal adventure playgrounds for the older lads, decades before that phrase had been coined. They would climb the ladders to the tops of the straw ricks and then slide down, and what I recall as much as anything was the free rein they were given to do that kind of thing. The 1920s were not noted for being soft on children, for whom a belt around the ear-hole from some adult or other in authority was almost an occupational hazard; but I remember those Evesham youngsters being given a marvellous time of it, and when, eventually, Auntie Lucy had boiled the water and brewed the urns of tea, teachers fetched a can of milk fresh from the cows to go with it as they settled down to their meal by the pond. So the day passed, and those who were stung by nettles while retrieving a ball were soothed by the teachers with the help of that most ancient of all country remedies, the dock leaf.

It was not just the Sunday schools that took to pastures new for the day, of course. Summer outings by train and charabanc were frequent and popular in the days before holidays with pay, and while Weston-super-Mare coupled with a steamer trip to South Wales was always a favourite, many groups set their sights farther afield. The local council road men seemed to favour Southend, and there was a famous story about a chap called Alf who lost his companion in London on their way home. He stopped a policeman in Piccadilly Circus and asked: 'Have you seen Dennis Taylor, a short, stiff chap in brown jacket and grey flannels, smoking a pipe?'

The policeman snorted: 'There are thousands of people here. How could I tell you if I'd seen him.' At which it was Alf's turn to snort, letting it be known that in Pershore, where he came from, no bobby worth his salt would be unaware of any new face in town.

Uncle George went every summer to Scarborough or Ilfracombe for a long day's outing. You reached Ilfracombe by train to Sharpness in Gloucestershire and then by steamer down the Bristol Channel; but Scarborough was a different matter altogether, for it was three o'clock in the morning when the excursion left our village station. He went with some friends from Evesham, who apparently could teach even the Yorkshiremen of 'the Queen of the Watering Places' a thing or two about tight-fistedness. One year, growing increasingly ravenous, they looked at the menu posted up outside nearly every café in Scarborough, only for my uncle's friend Bill to complain that the prices were too high for dinner. At last they saw a notice that read: 'A good dinner for eightpence.' They went in and Uncle George, who liked peas as all countrymen do, complained that the ones served were as hard as bullets. Every time he and his friends tried to eat them with their forks, they shot off their plates. 'These peas have been here all the season, no doubt,' Uncle George grumbled as Bill lifted his plate to his mouth to make sure he had mopped up every spot of gravy. And as they left, he turned to the queue enticed by the promise of a good dinner for eightpence and pronounced: 'A good dinner indeed! If you want peas as hard as bullets, this is the place!'

Another red letter day was the annual club feast, when members of the Sick and Dividend Club paraded to church in the morning. The officials carried long sticks with brass figures on the handles, and the farmers put jugs of beer and cider on the walls in readiness for the men as they walked back from the service to a marquee in the Plough and Harrow yard, where there was a spread of prime beef, ham, pickles and apple pies. Men who had paid a few coppers every month now shared the bounty of the money left over after sickness benefits had been paid out, and after the feasting there were coconut shies and other attractions for all. One year a villager called Ern took my nineteen-year-old cousin Nellie from London high above the plum trees in a swingboat, but he

Traveller's rest: rootless people descended on farms from far and wide at harvest time

The gypsies' close-knit and complex family ties often baffled the farmers who employed them

grew anxious as her face paled after a day of romping and feasting in the village. 'Bist a feeling sick?' he asked in his unembroidered local brogue.

'Just a traiful,' she replied in her new-fangled London way, and soon he had lowered the boat and taken her to sit and listen to the band through the long, warm evening.

What a boon those village high days were in those pre-National Health days, a tonic for all. 'Only another eleven months, two weeks and a fort-night to go to the next Ashton Club,' a friend of my father joked as they were packing the stalls away for another year, and there was an element of truth in it. On Monday morning it would be back with a vengeance to the old routine. On wet days in July the village men mended and painted the fruit-picking ladders, for by the first days of the month the early hay plums were already ripe and yellow on the orchard trees. When it rained I would often take a couple of horses for shoeing at the blacksmith at Sedgeberrow. Riding the foremost horse with the other's halter tied to his tail, I went the two miles along what was then a quiet lane to the neigh-bouring village, where I invariably found the smith busy, for wet days in the summer always saw his services in great demand. So it would be a waiting game with the boys from the other farms, and we would marvel at the strength of the blacksmith. Dressed in strong corduroy trousers, thick shirt and a heavy leather apron, he would lift a horse's hoof and tuck its leg between his own with no apparent effort. As a special treat, he would allow us to paint black oily liquid on the newly-shod hooves to smarten them up for the journey home.

The fact is that unsettled weather is very often a feature of mid-July – which gives an added edge to the old threat that if it rains on St Swithin's Day, 15 July, it will do so for the next forty. I do not think we believed this old tale in the Vale of Evesham any more or less than folk did in any other part of the country – but we felt a close affinity with that other name for the 15th, Apple Christening Day. They say that long before my time it was considered very wrong to pick the fruit before the saint's day – though it is debatable how much this was down to old Swithin, or Swithun as his name is more usually spelled these days. Some said that the flavour of apples would be affected if you jumped the gun, but we must face the fact that in Britain, apples are normally unfit to be picked before that date, anyway. Oh, yes, little boys have been known to scrump the fruit green from the orchards well before then, but their exploits are usually followed by stomach ache. I remember picking Beauty of Bath apples just after Apple Christening Day one year, and though they were not quite ripe, they were not at all bad to eat. The men with the ladders would pick the early Ecklinville cooking apples soon after that date, too. That particular species is no longer grown in Worcestershire, but it was a good early cooker produced often from cankered and unpromising looking trees.

As for the hot days, the days when the smith would be casting around for work, you could almost see the corn ripening in the fields, and even the birds would not muster the energy to sing. 'Tis dog days,' the old folk would say. 'Now don't play about with the dogs, because they be miserable.' It was true; the dogs retreated to shady places in the stone-slabbed kitchen when the sun burned up the ground. The village cricketers and their spectators found little fault with a warm, dry July, however, and the sun on Mr Tandy's carefully prepared greensward was a glorious sight. Those were the days when the batsmen were the kings of cricket, with wickets prepared with scant regard for giving the bowlers an even break, and that philosophy seeped right down to the grass roots of the game. It was good to see 300 runs scored on a Saturday afternoon, whoever won the day. It was also a grand break from the fields, whether you were playing or merely spectating. Some say that July should bring farmers and their men a break between haymaking and harvest, but I've never been aware of any such luxury. I still reckon it is one of the busiest months of the year.

CHAPTER EIGHT

August

Moonlight and Fakeums

August in the country is a time of gathering, and it is a month when some of our migrant birds begin to depart. The swallows and martins start to congregate, while the swifts start their long journey south. The song birds resume their tuneful singing after the relative silence of hot July. It's good that some rural communities have again adopted the old custom of harvest suppers. Anyone who cherishes the colourful traditions of old village life must try to imagine the scene at the old harvest home when, by lantern light in a timbered barn, the men of the land ate, drank, sang and told their tales, waited on by the farmer and his family. I remember being told that after a good harvest during the Boer War, there was a memorable harvest home in John Crump's big barn in my village of Ashton-under-Hill. One of the dances, the Rose Basket, was accompanied by the waving of handkerchiefs while the assembled company sang Sweet Annie Benbow. John Drinkwater, the Midlands poet who was part of that coterie that gathered in the North Gloucestershire village of Dymock in the years before the First World War, jotted down some of the old rustic tunes, and at that party Charles the carter recited one of them:

> All ye rakish farmers that stay up late at night,
> Mind when you go to bed choose some candlelight.
> Now Betty you go up to bed
> And I'll stay up tonight instead.

The traditional harvest home is much more ancient than the church harvest festival, which was one of the many inventions of enterprising Victorian clergymen. Stephen Hawker, the eccentric vicar of the

Cornish village of Morwenstow, conducted the first harvest festival in the 1840s – and bearing in mind the hardships of that decade, with the Irish potato famine at its height, thanks for harvests safely gathered in was doubtless heartfelt in a way that it rarely is in this country today. Nevertheless, it always seems a pity to me that there are no longer harvest home celebrations in village barns. The spontaneous songs of the harvester and his wife, the beef and the ham and the ale, were surely a 'thank you' to the men who had laboured hard and long on the land. I often wonder why this business of saying 'thank you' to the Almighty could not have somehow been coupled with this. I see harvesting as a classic partnership between the toiler in the field and his God, and personally I say thank you to both.

What was certainly heaven-sent – or at least a gift of the starry heights – was the harvest moon by which the farm folk of old set up their stooks of corn in rows long after nightfall. But all through the year the moon was a very good friend to country people, in both their work and play. Many village social events were timed to coincide with a full moon, so that those out late could walk or even drive home by its rays, rather than by the cloudy light of a lantern or rush candles. And many an Evesham market gardener would work the clay with his two-tine digger under a brilliant moon after the winter frosts had cemented the top spit. Until the black-outs of the last war, people in big towns and cities had never appreciated the light of the moon and stars, but their value was not lost on that great country author Wentworth Day, who wrote: 'Riding a horse at night is one of the greatest joys on earth. The world and the scents of the night are yours – all the white witchery of the moon and old, gaunt trees.' I knew a man who had experienced that sensation at first hand – though without the benefit of the moonlight! Towards the end of his long life, Percy Attwood, born in 1874, said to me: 'Have you ever ridden a pony on a dark night? As a boy of twelve I used to ride to Evesham and back, about fifteen miles, for music lessons. Do you know the wide grass verge by the Hinton turn? There was a grip, there, a trench to take the surface water off the road. I was cantering along that verge one dark night and my pony jumped high in the air, just to clear the grip. It was a strange sensation, jumping in the dark.' Our grandfathers always planted their crops according to the phases of the moon. They killed their pigs when it was waxing because it was said that if you did the job when it was on the wane, all the bacon would fry away to nothing in the pan. As for the hunter's moon, the one that follows the harvest, it was always a blessing after a hard day with the chase to ride home with the horse ambling wearily along the white-lit path.

In the hours between work and the final waning of the light I used to spend some August evenings watching Jack Hunting making pegs for rabbit wires out of straight-grained ash wood. He worked in a thatched barn and was known as a rough carpenter, but I thought him a craftsman. His tools were sharp and his eye was keen. 'These pegs are to hold the necklaces for the rabbits on Bredon Hill,' he would say. Then he spun the copper or brass wire into snares. Brightly they shone until Jack held them over a smoky wood fire to dull them from reflecting the moonlight. I knew how clever he was with his snares. On a beam above his bench hung a stick with a dozen young rabbits paunched ready for sale. 'Got them with me twelve-bore when the binder cut the oats on the hill,' he said. 'I reckon the gaffer paunched a hundred or more.' There is something special about the taste of rabbit three-parts grown from a cornfield – and there was certainly no shortage of them in our part of the country in those days. Indeed, there is no shortage of them now, for the species has bounced back spectacularly, and perhaps predictably, after the great myxomatosis plague of the mid-1950s. In the old days I have seen Bredon Hill literally moving with rabbits, and I firmly believe a friend of mine who said he once caught 10,000 in a season. He shot at one rabbit near some burrows, or holts as we called them, and killed four. Their liking for the comparatively poor hill country is not surprising, for lush, green grass kills rabbits, but it is remarkable how our local warrens were known far and wide. The tale is told of Squire Parsons, an eighteenth-century landowner from Kemerton, walking through the streets of London and being amazed by a street vendor's proud cry of: 'Bredon Hill rabbits!'

At the time Jack Hunting was making his snares, there was considerable debate about methods of catching rabbits. In 1937 a House of Lords Select Committee met to consider the damage to crops by them, and there was much interesting evidence from one farmer, David Perkins. He said that in spite of killing five thousand of them with gin

Hops were an important crop not only in Kent but in my native south-west Midlands

traps in 1926, he failed to reduce their numbers on his farm in the following year. So he started ferreting instead, and in three years he had
cleared his farm of rabbits. Perkins noticed that out of every nine rabbits
killed either by ferrets or by his gun as they bolted, seven were does.
When traps had been used, they caught far more of the venturesome
bucks, which would be first out of the burrow at night; they also killed
stoats and weasels, which lived on the rabbits, so one way and another,
the does were left comparatively safe in the burrows to breed. And as we
have rediscovered in recent years, they breed quickly.

Not that Jack's skills with wood began and ended with snares. 'I've
made you a ladder,' he said to me one August day. 'It's time you started
plum picking. This un's fifteen rung, just right for you, bwoy.' Admiring
his workmanship, I lifted it out on to the grass in front of the barn. 'See
this un?' he said with a laugh, pointing out the shortest ladder I had
ever seen. 'Made for blackberry picking – only six rungs!' With Jack
there was the feeling of being in the presence of a man who was far
from ordinary. As I came away from the barn he called out: 'Did you
ever hear of Tommy Dyke and his watercress ladder? Only three rungs

long, and he stood on the middle un to pick watercress.' A kind man, was Jack, and his leg-pulls were inimitable.

He was not alone, however, in his skills, and it is certainly true that there is nothing new about 'do-it-yourself'. Countrymen have always had an eye for improvisation, and we even had a name for the products of their versatility; we called them 'fakeums'. The mower who needed a new sned or handle for his scythe would look for a growing branch in the hedge. He knew what twisted shape that branch had to be. Traps for sparrows were easily adapted from a riddle or sieve propped up with a short stick attached to a long piece of binder twine. A little chaff or corn was placed under the riddle on a cold, snowy winter's day, and the birds were lured away from stealing the fowl corn. One snatch on the twine from the barn doorway, and the sparrow was trapped. Rabbit snares made from six strands of brass wire could be bought in the iron-mongers, but the Bredon Hill rabbits were strong, and broke them. Jack made his from eight strands, and spun a lead weight from the bottom of the wires, which were suspended from a beam in his workshop. Our old carpenter made mallets, beetles or bittles from straight pieces of crab apple wood, bored a hole in the rounded side and then put in an ash handle. Good, they were, for driving in hedge stakes. A knife for cutting or trimming straw thatch was made from an old scythe blade, and not many men bought setting pins for planting sprouts and cabbages. Some cut an L-shaped stick from the hedge and used a pocket knife to sharpen the point; others used the broken crutch or handle of a fork or spade.

Then there were what we knew as 'tempories'. When the horse plough wheel slipped and the set screw could not be tightened any more, the stem of the wheel was prevented from moving in the iron collar by a cart nail driven home between the stem and the collar with a plough spanner. Most plough spanners had a hammer head at one end and a spike at the other, all made from iron. The spike was slipped into set screws to tighten them, and the hammer, known as a Brummagem spanner, had many uses. Market gardeners used pieces of ash wood to make rakes, driving in a row of six-inch nails to make the head. The distance between the nails depended on how finely the gardener wished to rake the soil. A hole would be bored through the middle of the head, and a round ash stick inserted in it for the handle. Primitive bird scarers on strawberry patches were made from little windmills and pieces of tin, so that the mill clanked the metal as it revolved.

I reckon that if a shopkeeper were asked for a putcheon today he would be confused. They were made of small seed bags with half of one side cut away, leaving an apron with a shallow bag to hold beans for setting. It would be tied around the waist and the worker would take the beans from the bag with his left hand and plant them with the setting pin in his right. A scratter is still a common tool among the market gardeners, though they call it a chrome in East Anglia. The early ones were made by blacksmiths by turning the tines of a partly worn-out fork at right-angles, and then using it as a heavy, narrow rake. I am sure that men on the land still invent tools for their own use, but the need is not so acute as it was at one time. 'Needs must when the devil drives' is a saying that is still true today. Fakeums and do-it-yourself inventions continue to fascinate me, and I often recall the favourite answer I received if I inquired about the origin of a particularly puzzling home-made article when I was a boy. 'Ah, it's a whim-wham off a mustard mill,' the old folk would say.

In the plum orchard where the men were using longer ladders I learned how to set my fifteen-runger in the fork of a tree. With a peck basket hung from a belt, there were good pickings to be had up among the leafy Victorias; and sometimes, when the harvest was too plenteous, the labourers left the Golden Pershores to rot and be eaten by wasps on the ground. At times like that the cry was:

> You ask me where and whence I come?
> Pershore, God help us;
> Don't ask about the crops at home,
> God help us;
> Last April, every sprig and spray
> Was deck'd with pearly blossoms gay.
> Last August, every branch and bough
> Was bent with yellow plums,
> But now, God help us!

That was the way it was. In a good plum year, it was the Land of Plenty. In a poor year it was Pershore, God help us! It was frustrating to see fruit wasting in that way, with nature's abundance defeating the efforts of even the largest of work-forces. Pershore was considered to be the centre for plum growing, and here the fruit men, both big and small, relied on the crop as a banker for the rest of the year. There has always been a certain amount of jesting about these men and their way of life. They were people who knew their job inside-out, but their conversation was so often tinged with a kind of fatalism. When a spring frost had threatened the crop, their world was seemingly at an end: 'It's killed the lot'; 'It's swept the deck'; 'It's almost killed the hovels'. These words and gloomier were uttered in the fruit markets of the 1920s when a late frost had blackened the blossom. So the men joked among themselves,

Harvesting with a scythe, a back-breaking operation still recalled by old farm hands in my young days

dreading the worst, and planted marrows for the jam-makers. Marrows would always sell in a bad plum year, to replace the fruit. I have heard it said: 'They'll be fishing the plum growers out of the Avon now the frost has got the blossom.' I do not know whether any disappointed and disillusioned men really did ever get around to taking the fatal plunge, but I knew one who, after a late frost, sat by his hovel all day long muttering to passers-by: 'It's killed the lot. It just wants an earthquake, now, to swallow us all up.'

The plum season lasts from late July to late October, with a much longer period for picking than most fruit. The withy-made pot hampers, which held seventy-two pounds of Pershore egg plums picked a bit on the green side, are long since gone. Victorias for dessert were packed in twelve-pound 'chips'. Today, so many varieties have gone from the orchards of the Vale. I am thinking in particular of Jimmy Moore and Cox's Emperor, with a flavour to beat all the peaches of the Mediterranean. But nothing has ever surpassed the Victoria for marketing, and as a coloured plum its flavour is supreme. It is odd how folk like coloured plums, as they do brown eggs. A really delicious yellow variety is the Warwickshire Drooper, which grows, like the egg plum, from its own suckers. It is also a good sort on which to graft other varieties. In the 1920s I remember seeing the original tree known as the Evesham Wonder, a throwback from the Pershore egg plum but red in colour. The grafts from this were put on egg plum stock and sold around the Vale, producing quite handsome fruit tasting exactly like the egg. It could not compete with the Victoria but produced nicely coloured fruit compared with the egg plum. A risky crop, are plums, but I can recall men who were daring enough, some years ago, to buy the crop on the trees, sometimes when the blossom was still out. I had an uncle who was such a man, and he was known in Evesham as the Plum King. He must have been successful, at least for some seasons, for he retired comfortably to Weston-super-Mare before he was fifty! A plum season gamble of a very different kind was made many years ago by Jimmy Partington, an old friend of mine who prided himself on being a judge of horse flesh. One day he noticed a likely looking gelding pulling a dray-load of plums to Pershore station, and something about the way it moved impressed him. After haggling with the grower about the price, beating him down from fifty pounds to forty-five guineas, he took the plunge – and landed himself the best horse he ever rode. He named it, somewhat eccentrically, KBO – Keep Buggering On! – and won with it at point-to-points and in an amateur race at Cheltenham. When I met him in later life, we always greeted each other with a triumphant KBO! With that kind of speedy pedigree, it is odd that he was best known in his last years as just about the slowest, most obstructive car driver in the Vale.

But plums aside, what huge numbers of people used to gather on the land at the peak of the annual rounds of harvests. Looking back over the years to when the sickle was used to cut the corn, you could scarcely have agreed with St Matthew's holy writ that told us that while the harvest was plenteous, the labourers were few. In the days before the mechanical reaper, wheat and oats were cut with a bagging hook and barley with a scythe. By hook and by crook, harvesting cost the farmer 12s an acre at the turn of the century, while cutting with the self-binder was estimated to cost 5s 2d. It was quite eye-catching to watch a man using two hooks to perfection. The one used with the bagging hook to pull out the sheaf was known as a pick-thank – a term that also described a cantankerous woman! We miss today the sight of stooks of sheaves standing up in rows like the aisles of a church, but no doubt our grandfathers had similar thoughts when the binder came along and there was no longer any need for men to use hooks.

As for the mushroom-like staddle stones on which we built the ricks, how little we dreamed then that before the end of the century they would be reduced to the status of garden ornaments – very decorative ones, I might add, and certainly very expensive ones. In fact the ones we used came in both round and rectangular form, and I expect most people know that they were made in that shape to keep the rats and mice from running up them into the ricks. At much the same time, seamen put cones on the ropes of ships when they were docked, wider end towards the shore, for the very same purpose. The staddle stones kept the unthreshed corn high off the damp floor of the rick yard, perhaps for up to six months, when corn prices were higher, and there was quite an art in making this foundation safe. In the first place, the stones were put in position in a circle or at the four corners of a rectangular

Loading stooks before the slow journey back to the rick yard

rick, when a further dozen would be brought in to fill the spaces in between them. Timbers were laid from stone to stone to form a framework, and smaller timbers and faggots of wood would be added to strengthen the base. The builder started his rick by making a stook of sheaves in the middle of the staddle, with the ears of corn uppermost, and then he followed round and round with the first course until he came to the edge of the rick. The next course he laid was started from the outside, with the butt ends of the straw facing outwards, and he would bind every row with the next row. This would continue until the rick was high enough for the roof to be put on – a weatherproof roof built in a special way. The middle of the rick was first filled with sheaves placed as before, but with the successive courses 'pulled in', or several inches short of the previous one. Then the builder would walk round this pyramid shape, placing the last sheaves in rows with the butt ends pointing down and the ears pointing to the apex of a round rick or the ridge of a rectangular one. These final sheaves formed a kind of thatch which would shoot off rain water before a skilled thatcher came to complete the job.

Springtime in the orchard, when new arrivals made the life of the farmer's wife even busier than usual

The cart was an integral part of the farmyard scene and the farmer's life

I used to look forward keenly to the visit of Tom the thatcher, whether it was for the hay ricks in summer or the straw in autumn. The thatching of our sainfoin clover rick on Bredon Hill was usually his first job for us, and after it had settled he would put a few boltings of straw along the ridge. My job was to cut the two strings of binder twine and draw the straw. Grasping an armful and putting it across my knees, I worked with both hands, straightening the thatching straw and making another bundle from the loose bits of cavings or weeds. Tom stuck a row of pegs in a staggered line from the ridge to the eaves of the rick, staggered so that when he had fixed the thatching on them, the rain would not penetrate by running in a straight line down the roof. Another of my jobs was to make a heap of withy sticks into these pegs. This I did with a billhook and chopping block, cutting, splitting and pointing the pegs to the right size. Short pegs were used for the hay ricks, and long for the corn. Tom made such a tidy job of his thatching that it always seemed a pity to take the thatch off, when the hay had to be cut for the cattle or the corn threshed.

In this way, the rick was secure from top to toe, though farmers had to take extra precautions to keep their corn harvest free from rats and mice, which always found the thought of a nest in the straw enticing when the cold weather set in. The rick ladder always had to be moved away, of course; and a man who worked for me many years ago told me that when he was a boy, he was sent to the yard at harvest time to crawl under the ricks with a pair of sheep shears and clip all the straws hanging down to the ground. These would be quite enough, he explained, to give rats and mice a convenient ladder up into the rick.

That is all a world away from the golden stone mushrooms seen in the immaculately tended grounds of big Cotswold houses today. But the sight of staddles still brings back memories of those hard-working men who built the ricks, just as the sunshine in cottage gardens at this time of year often reminds me of Bunch Baldwyn, something of a legendary character in our village in the 1920s. A caring lady of the right kind, she worked anonymously and secretly, and no one will ever know the extent of her kindness to the sick and poor. I suppose she could have been called a sort of unpaid social worker pottering along from cottage to cottage with jellies, blancmanges and beef tea, but her greatest gift was simply her presence. She always remembered people in their hour of need, and that is what mattered most of all. Bunch never married, but she lived in one of our farm cottages, and when she came to pay her rent she often related stories of her experiences of love with the captain of the local fire brigade. To me her tales were sheer entertainment on those pre-radio winter nights. She was a kind eccentric, but how much poorer would life have been without her. She would spend whole summer days in her garden, where the crowded flowers struggled for existence with their neighbours. She had an enormous collection of crockery, and more often than not her dirty cups and saucers and plates remained in the sink and round about for long periods, awaiting the great day when she would suddenly have a blitz on her washing-up.

Agile little Bunch was a member of a family who had lived as landowners and farmers for 600 years. Her father Thomas Baldwyn built Rockland House in the time of William IV, about 1830, and it was a fine three-storey dwelling for his family. Farming, though, has always been a male-dominated calling, and it was seen as a devastating blow to the family fortunes when Bunch's brother died in his youth, leaving only Thomas's three daughters surviving. Bunch set about learning the principles of nursing from one Dr Wellington, and she could diagnose illness and apply medicines and poultices quite independently. The occasional mistake did occur, of course, and Jack, our rough carpenter, suffered more from the treatment than from the ailment, once, when a mustard plaster for his rheumatic back was applied a little on the hot side. Another memory of her was her habit of inviting the bell ringers to her cottage after midnight on New Year's morning. They would solemnly walk through the house, drink her health and wish her a happy new year.

As an accomplished organist, she played at the parish church for many years – and also at a neighbouring church, where she always and perhaps wishfully claimed that the bachelor parson was a bit sweet on her. She excelled at funerals, her *pièce de résistance* being the Dead March from Saul. There always seemed to be a certain resonance in our church for the bass notes in this music. Every pew and every timber seemed to respond to Bunch's playing – solemn, very loud and with the little boy organ-blower at full stretch. She also ran a very tolerant Mothers'

Safely gathered in: the apple harvest comes home

Union, where all women were equal and no one was more equal than anyone else. Bunch feared no person, and once told an over-industrious keeper of the churchyard that he was making graves look like marrow beds and that she had more bones buried there than he had. It was all in good spirit, though, for he used her bass brooms, borrowed her wheelbarrow, drank her cups of tea and shared the cakes she often made. One thing that did frighten her was thunder, and I remember her inviting my sister to stay with her in her cottage one stormy night, coaxing her to sleep with trifles. She kept up her own spirits with the aid of a fair-sized bottle of Woodpecker cider! On one sultry August afternoon I was walking past her cottage with our cowman when she greeted us with: 'What a lovely day.'

'Yes, Ma'am,' replied Tom, with his usual dry wit, 'but I reckon we shall have some tempest tonight.' He went on his way chuckling, knowing he had struck the Achilles heel of this great little lady who gave the village folk so much help, health and happiness.

CHAPTER NINE

September

All Good Gifts Around Us

When this time of year comes around I always think back to the harvest festival in our chapel in 1926, when I was eleven. The pews were packed, and as well as the usual awesome display of fruit and vegetables, our Sunday school superintendent, James Cotton, had combined the skill of his hands with his fertile imagination to put on a display consisting of a wheat rick on carved wooden staddle stones, a lump of coal and a glass of water. I presume that, as always, the sermon was on the 'harvest of souls' theme, the separation of the wheat from the chaff. But how heartily we sang 'All is safely gathered in', in that village where so much of what we ate came from the orchards and fields around us. Not, perhaps, that all was quite as simple as it seemed, in this cross between a church service and a produce show. The giant pumpkins and gourds, fed with liquid manure all the summer, were often grown in competition by some members of the congregation. The vegetable marrows, given pride of place in the front of the display, had had their yellow or green skins scratched with biblical texts when they were still maturing, and the messages became writ ever larger as the vegetables swelled. 'We shall come rejoicing, bringing in the sheaves' is one I remember.

Out in the countryside, of course, the harvest goes on all the year round. The best of the plums are over by the time the cereal crops are ripe, but with bread having a special significance to the church as both the body of Christ and the staff of life, it is perhaps not surprising that it celebrates harvest festival after the corn has been safely gathered in. I used to enjoy the Monday harvest service, as well. This was held the day after the main event, and once again the choir sang an anthem while the fruit still lay on the window sills and around the pulpit. I recall the yellow eyes of the potatoes peeping at me from the scrubbed white tubers in the golden glow of the paraffin lamps. This latter service was not too long, and after it we would gather in the vestry for the produce to be auctioned for some good cause or other. We had walked up the village street with our peck baskets, following the older members of the chapel with their candle lanterns, and we had a shilling or so in our pockets. Apples, walnuts and damsons were, of course, everyday autumn fare for us; it was something special we were after, a section of honeycomb or perhaps a bunch of grapes. The problem was, such delicacies usually went for more than we could afford, and so our chance would slip away for another year. At last the final bunch of beetroot would go under the hammer, there would be an announcement that the eggs would be going along to the local hospital, and that was the end of harvest festival for another year. The chapel was now naked of produce, with just a few of the more robust flowers left on the pulpit ready for the following Sunday; once more the yearly ritual of saying 'thank you' was over.

Not that all the beauties of the earth are restricted to the vegetable kingdom in autumn, for this is the season when the ground is often covered with spiders' webs, spun from shrub to shrub or simply floating in the air. This silken substance, known as gossamer, is the work of an infinite number of small spiders and has never been described more memorably than by Gilbert White of Selborne:

On September the 21st I rose before daybreak and I found the stubbles and clover grounds matted all over with a thick coat of cobwebs, in the meshes of which a copious and heavy dew hung so plentifully that the whole face of the country seemed as it were covered with two or three setting nets drawn one over another. When the dogs attempted to hunt, their eyes were so blinded and hoodwinked that they could not proceed, but were obliged to lie down and scrape the encumbrances from their faces with their forefeet. As the morning advanced, the sun became bright and the day turned to one of those most lovely ones which no season but autumn produces.

What memories are revived by this observation by White, memories of the maxims of stockmen of many years ago. The yearly incidence of husk or hoose in cattle was attributed to cobwebs on the September pasture. Early morning stillness exaggerates sounds in the fields, and the hacking cough of yearling cattle suffering from husk is more of a bark, as guttural as the call of a stag at rutting time. It seemed sensible for the stockman to yard the young beasts away from the dewy brookside meadows, but in truth the ailment had nothing to do with cobwebs. The problem was a worm in the windpipe, part of the life cycle of the *strongylus micrurus* snail – but since this was particularly troublesome on low, badly drained lands liable to flooding, the sort of country in which gossamer would be most apparent in the early morning dew, perhaps the cattle men of old were not so off-beam in letting the spiders' very visible legacy warn them off fields favoured by the far less visible snails.

I smile sometimes when I recall that when no apparent reason could be found for disease or loss in cattle or sheep, some old idea – a kind of agricultural folklore – would provide a name for the cause of the trouble. I wonder for how many hundred years the sudden death of a month-old lamb frothing at the mouth was said to be wool in the maw, or a result of the lamb pulling wool off the hedges and getting it curdled with the milk. It no doubt happens, but as often as not the cause of death is pulpy kidney disease. Whatever, I spent many an hour of my youth tugging wool off the bars of rough hurdles to prevent lambs from swallowing it, and I wonder now whether it was really so necessary. Lighter by far than the wisps of oily wool were the thistledown and the beautiful winged seed of the dandelion as they floated along on their voyage of discovery. Goldfinches certainly enjoyed this harvest of the thistles, while bees settled on the still purple blossom.

September in the fields is a rich month. The grass grows well, although the old men used to say 'There's not the stay in it,' and I have seen the stockman carry kibbled cotton cake to sawn-off nine-gallon cider barrels in the field, and watched the cattle enjoy this supplement to their diet from these improvised troughs. September sometimes also brought a second mowing of broad red clover – an aftermath, in the original sense of the word, though in Worcestershire we were more prone to calling it a lattermath. In the orchards the men would be

Back to school: after long weeks in the harvest fields, country children often found it hard to re-adapt to classroom routine

picking the apples – not the keepers, but the early cookers and Worcesters for eating. Some of those early cooking apples had a texture and flavour of their own. Ecklinville was eaten raw and was 'as sour as varges', but as a cooker, did any apple taste so good in September or go to such a delectable froth in the saucepan? It is a pity it was such a scabby tree, full of canker. Apples in the village were both overhead and underfoot when I was a boy. They were taken for granted. I have seen pigs running in the orchards eating Great Warner King apples fallen by the gales. The old rhyme is so true:

> At Michaelmas or a little before
> Half the apple's thrown away with the core.
> At Christmas time or a little bit after
> If it's sour as a crab
> It's thank you, master.

What a pity the coveys of September partridges are so rare these days. The whirr of their wings as they fly from the stubbles always fascinates me, and the metallic clinking sound they make from the furrows at evening time as they call the younger members of the brood always speaks of autumn. Time was when the netting of partridges on the September stubbles was common, a practice referred to in a poem by Pope, and I have seen hawthorn and furze bushes scattered wide over the bare cornfields to prevent this kind of poaching at night.

'How's thee taters turning out?' was a question asked so often from the bench in the harness room of the stable. The carter depended so much on the yield of his crop on the headland. In fact it was the topic of conversation from Good Friday planting to the lifting in the autumn.

'Mine be the finest in the village,' the shepherd replied. It was a statement soon questioned by the carter after a particularly dry summer, until the shepherd added: 'If they were much finer you would hardly see them; they be like marbles!' It is difficult to believe today that in the 1920s some families would eat a ton of potatoes a year. Fashions and needs change. I have seen men eat daily the top of a cottage loaf and a hunk of cheese for their ten o'clock 'bait', to follow that with fat boiled bacon for their midday dinner, along with a lump of bread pudding. This was when the work in the fields all depended on the power of horses and men.

Men of real power remembered by me at this fruit-picking time of year are Pietro and Giuseppe, Peter and Joe, two of a number of Italian prisoners-of-war from a camp near Winchcombe who worked on our farm in the 1940s. Peter had been a vine grower near Naples, and he was a handy man to have on the land, while Joe, a factory worker, made up for his ignorance of country life by his strength. Sacks of wheat weighing two-and-a-quarter hundredweight were absolutely no problem for him. The men spoke a little English, Peter reasonably well. I asked him one day when we were haymaking why he did not play football with the other men at weekends and he replied: 'Boss, if I break my leg, do you think Mr Churchill will give me another one? My mother is very old, and she wants to see me again. It's not possible for her to make another Pietro.' This was one of the finest examples of a logic which I came to admire. He told me that the prisoners would discuss their farmer bosses on their lorry every morning: 'Mr Smith very good boss, plenty work; Mr Brown no good, treat us badly so we go slow, slow.'

This proved to me the truth of the old saying that you can lead but not drive, and it reinforced my view that it was a good policy to treat the men with fairness. If I had to go to Gloucester Market to buy calves on a Monday, I would tell the Italians what to do before I left. Maybe it was hoeing sprouts; whatever it was, they did as much work in my absence as they would have done if I had been there.

'What do we do, boss, when we have finished that field?' Joe would say.

'Pick some apples in the orchard where you worked the other day,' I would reply.

'Sure, boss, we will. Could you bring us some Players please from the market?' A packet of Players guaranteed a lot of work.

In the orchard I had two Pitmaston Duchess pear trees. They were really tall, and we had to borrow a forty-rung ladder from a neighbour for the men to pick the fruit. The wind was blowing almost a gale on one occasion, and I told Peter to pick the pears and Joe to stand on the bottom of the ladder to steady it. This idea did not appeal to him at all. 'What do you think the people of Ashton-under-Hill would say about me, boss?' he said. 'Lazy devil, no doubt. I want another ladder. Pietro's

Buying and selling sheep was always a feature of the September scene

all right up the long one by himself.' I can still see Peter swaying in the wind, picking those pears at the top of the tree, and Joe doing the same among the lower branches. They became so much a part of our life that after a few months they asked if I would billet them on the farm. 'Next to the pigsties, that little cart house would do us nicely, boss,' they said eagerly. With a little range fitted alongside one wall, two camp beds, a table, two chairs and an oil lamp, the Italians were installed in their new home. When I fetched them from camp I had to sign a sort of conveyance note, and I can still remember its wording: 'Today I have received the live body of Pietro Pedalino and Giuseppe Claridi. Signed Fred Archer . . .' Happily, our relationship continued to flourish after they had moved in. They were easy to cater for and did not mind the meat shortage. If they had potatoes, macaroni, beans and bread they were quite happy. They grew tomatoes and peppers in the garden, and used margarine for cooking. At a shilling an hour, paid to the war agricultural committee, and up those lofty pear trees, their faces exhilarated by the blustery wind and their precarious perches, they gave me a September memory of the wartime years that lives with me to this day.

Peter and Joe could also rustle up a meal out of the mushrooms we would find on our way home from the fields at this time of year – but so could we all, with the big ones, known as horse mushrooms, used for making ketchup, and the small ones for frying. The field mushroom always seems to have so much more flavour than those grown indoors.

As September ended it was the time of the sheep fairs, and our shepherd turned out the rams. With hand shears he had already clipped the ewes' tails, giving them a poodle dog look, to make mating easier; and then the ram would be raddled with a mixture of red ochre powder and linseed oil, made into a paste and plastered on to his chest so that we could see how many of the ewes had been served. In the traditional breeds, ewes take no interest in mating until the days shorten in September, the exception being the Dorset Horn; she would take the ram in May and lamb in October.

Michaelmas Day, 29 September, is known as the end of the farming year, the time when houses and land change hands. It is also a rent day –

and for this reason, it could be a busy time for threshing ricks of corn that had been left uncovered with thatch. Farmers would say that they needed to do this job for bedding or feed – but what they really meant was that they needed to sell the wheat for cash as the quarterly rent day loomed. But what of St Matthew's Day on 21 September? In Worcestershire we used to say:

On St Matthee
Shut up the bee.

Happy times, then, this month. And in October we could always look forward to St Luke's Little Summer.

CHAPTER TEN

October

Happiness was a Cottage Pig

After rough weather in late September had laid windfall apples like a green and gold carpet under the orchard trees, St Luke's Day on 18 October often heralded a period of almost summer-like weather. It always seemed to us that the warm days were loath to give way to the long hours of darkness and the rimy frosts of autumn. As welcome as the flowers in May are these days of respite. They have a feel about them akin to the ageing cricketer who returns to the crease for an end-of-season match. There is a feeling that the summer days are not quite over – and yes, fruits do mature under the late autumn sun. The damsons still on the trees give us a purple picture now the leaves are thick on the grass. Gathered like grapes from summer lands and the last of the plum family to be harvested, they blossomed early on the trees along with the blackthorn. Sloes, the blackthorn fruit, will stay on the leafless twigs awhile, food for free to be gathered at leisure. Traditionally, St Luke's Day was also the time to turn out the ram:

> On St Luke's Day
> Let the tup have play.

In the villages of the Avon Vale, October was always the month when men with sharp bagging hooks cut the red-berried bower on the asparagus beds. In my village I remember pitching the delicate fern on to a dray and taking it with other boys to Finches Piece, the mangold ground. I smile to think how many crops of mangolds, year after year, grew in Finches Piece. This field was chosen mainly because those three-and-a-half acres were within a short distance of the cattle yards and barns. We covered the mangold heap with asparagus bower in those

Fodder in store: another load of mangolds for the bury

days back in the 1930s when straw was scarcely to be found. It was a time when the land produced mainly cattle and sheep, and haymaking was the main harvest, apart from a small acreage of oats. The mangold heap in October was built two farm carts wide. The roots were tipped at one end, and stacked by the carter, Golden Tankard and Red Chief being two equally popular varieties. The heap, or bury, stood on the headland like a long terrace of cottages, thatched with asparagus fern to protect the fodder from the winter frosts.

After the crop had been allowed to sweat in the bury, the whole structure was covered with soil dug from a trench along its sides. I often think back to those mangold harvests, and remember how Dad competed for a silver cup awarded to the farmer who grew the heaviest crop. You had to grow a given number of acres from Carter's tested seeds, and I remember helping to plant some of these in a liberally manured bed under leaded lights on the headland. When the time came to send the giant mangolds by train to the seedsmen, we walked the long rows of roots in Finches Piece to see whether any of them had grown bigger than the ones given special attention under the frame. Yes, Dad won the cup that year, and we also had a beauty of a mangold to hollow out for a candle lantern at Hallowe'en. There seems to have been a revival of this tradition in recent years, a lot of it re-imported, I think, from the United States through the influence of film and television. I know that in those days long before television, watching the candle-lit images thrown by those gruesome faces was the best of fun – and I am sure those old Hallowe'en traditions used to sharpen the imagination of little children on dark nights.

I often feel that if you live in the country, among the hills and woods, you take the autumn tints on the trees for granted. Those many-coloured leaves of green turning yellow, bronze and red hang on in October until one morning when we wake to a white world of hoar frost; then they shower down, a gentle rain of foliage that has been shading the land since the spring. This was the time of year when the village worthies of my youth compared their pigs on Sunday mornings as they drank their cider or home-made wine. They leaned over the sty walls, holding their pint pots and sizing up the weight of bacon and meat to come. 'He's sixteen score, I reckon,' would be the estimate of George, the proud owner of a Gloucester Old Spot.

'No, never, I say about fifteen score,' his neighbour Harry, the barber, would reply. 'He unt such a pig as mine. Come and have a look at that un.' So round they would trot to Harry's, where one or two customers might be looking a little bit impatient.

'Shan't be a minute,' he would say. 'George has come to look at the pig, then I'll start cutting you chaps' hair.' They stared at the pig, muttered more estimated weights, and then Harry's wife would bring out the kitchen chair and put it on the garden path. The business of hair-cutting began, helped along by the odd glass of parsnip wine.

When Joe came from Conderton to kill the pigs he brought with him a steel yard, a primitive but accurate weighing machine that settled all the arguments. His perambulations around the Vale villages lasted from October until March, with a special flurry of activity just before Christmas, and the smoke from the burning of the pigs' bristles rose in cottage gardens through all the winter months. The Spanish say: 'On

St Luke's Day, kill your pigs and bung up your barrels.' But in our village the saint's day marked only the beginning of Joe's winter work, work that guaranteed a supply of delicious home-cured bacon to feed the men on the land during the colder breakfast mornings of the year.

Much has been written about the importance of the 'cottager's pig' in the village life of yesterday. The farm worker, whose wages for so long lagged behind those received, though not necessarily earned, by his cousin in the town, depended on a few simple possessions to enjoy a reasonable standard of living. His potatoes were one important mainstay; another was his pig in the cottage sty, fed on potato peelings, household scraps and other bits and pieces, all mixed together in what was known as the swill tub, or more accurately the pig wash barrel – often a cider barrel that had gone sour. This strong-smelling, soup-like fare was often supplemented by 'sharps' or 'middling' bought from the local baker. The pig supplied the villager with bacon, lard and meat for at least part of the year, and for a small fee he could even insure it against disease or premature death by joining the village pig club, a kind of National Insurance or social security scheme for these animals that were so vital to their owners' well-being. I have a rule book issued to members of a South Worcestershire pig club in the latter part of the last century. Rule one says that the object of the club is the insurance and relief of members who have the misfortune to lose a pig. Entrance fees varied: 'A member entering one or more store pigs shall pay one shilling entrance fee for each pig, and for every sow or boar pig, two shillings and sixpence. None shall be entered under nine weeks old, and should a member's boar die through castration, the owner shall be excluded from the benefit of the funds.' Generally speaking, if a member neglected his pig in any way whatever, he lost all rights to benefit. Another rule stated that 'every member shall pay one penny per week for each store pig so entered, and for every sow or boar, twopence per week.' The club in our village passed an interesting resolution at one of its meetings. These gatherings were presided over by three trustees, the president, treasurer and secretary, and were supported by a committee of management. It resolved that any member being in the club room in a state of intoxication should be fined sixpence for the first offence, a shilling for the second and a florin for the third.

Listening to the sermon: part of the weekly pattern of church and chapel life at a time when the 'Continental Sunday' was seen as a threat to British life

When harvesting was still a task for strong men and horses

The men on the buries lost no time in covering the mangolds with straw

It was the president's job to ear mark the pig after it was registered. If it then died through no fault of its owner he would receive ten shillings for each score of pounds, the weight being estimated by the committee. I remember a friend of mine had a fat pig that got sunstroke and died. He was paid the animal's value, but had to buy another small pig and start all over again. Anyone who was a jobber or dealer in pigs was not allowed to join the club, and no liquor or smoking was allowed in the club room while the serious business of meetings was taking place. Which breed did the cottagers favour? In our part of the world it was most definitely the Gloucester Old Spot, which thrived well on pig wash, sharps, cabbage and greens. In spring it was a common sight to see men gathering roadside grass and clovers to give their animals, while in autumn the windfall apples were relished, either fed in the sty or tipped into the wash barrel to mix with the other offal. If an Old Spot ever had the run of an orchard it thought it was in heaven, and people used to say that you could actually taste the fruit in the animal's meat;

they would joke that if you ate pork from an orchard pig you could save yourself the bother of making apple sauce. There was also a breed known as the Cottagers' Pig, a curly-coated white animal. And in later years club members favoured a cross between the Large White and the Large Black, which produced animals that were either black or an intriguing kind of blue and white. The pig clubs were revived in the war years, and by surrendering bacon coupons, a ration of balancer meal was allowed for a pig to be kept. This ration of pig food was bought in bulk by the club secretary and could be collected from the local baker, an arrangement that in some villages led to speculation over what went into his bread.

Even more seasonal than Joe's pig-killing was the spate of late-autumn mop or hiring fairs, which even by my childhood in the 1920s had been transformed into gatherings of mere pleasure. Long gone were the days when carters seeking a new master would go along with whipcord in their hat, shepherds would carry a piece of wool and local girls looking

Pigs in the orchard were a vital part of the local economy

to go into service would carry – yes – mops. But our old stockman once told me how the farm men used to save their extra harvesting money to buy watertight boots for the winter at the fair, and there was still talk of how almost every pub in Stratford cooked a beast outside in the street in the town's annual mop and bull roast. My old Uncle Jim told me of Zulus taken prisoner in the 1879 war against that people pulling faces at the crowds through barrel cages, and then there were wart charmers and quack doctors who would do everything from pulling teeth to lancing corns. Folk paid twopence to see such marvels as the smallest pony in the world and a horse with five legs, and an old friend of mine used to talk about Alsatian dogs in crates described as wolves from Siberia; that was long before the Alsatian became a known breed in this country, and longer still before it took on the more user-friendly name of the German shepherd dog. 'Come and see the horse with his head where his tail ought to be!' The showman who made this proud announcement enjoyed only limited success at Evesham Mop, for word soon got out that it was simply a nag with his tail in the manger and his head towards the crowd. They said that both man and horse had to beat a hasty retreat out of town after that particular catchpenny, but leaving tricks like that aside, it is no wonder that the mop fairs had come to be associated with fun and excitement long before their original hiring function had become extinct.

One thing that was always fascinating – almost like magic – at the fairs of my childhood was the music. I remember as a boy listening to the old steam organs, which always seemed to have such a haunting quality. And I can still smell those great traction engines; even the smoke from their funnels was easier on the nose than today's diesel fumes. I would step over the generator cables in the light of the pressurized oil lamps over the coconut shies, and the continuous patter of the cheap jacks always fascinated me. For the brave there were the switchbacks, and a great attraction for the village lads was always the cakewalk, with constantly lurching and swaying platforms that could be very dangerous to your constitution indeed after a couple of drinks. The same applied to the cauliflower-eared boxers in the booths, who had all seen better days but were still more than a match for young lads well primed with cider, who more often than not came off second best in front of their pals or girlfriend. I played safe, making sure that at least some of my pennies went on golden brandy snaps or home-made sweets, and when I did risk a gamble one night it did not do me a lot of good. I had been attracted by a crowd gathered round a man who was putting gold watches in an envelope, one after another. 'Anybody give me a shilling for this envelope?' he was shouting. There was silence until the envelope was opened and out fell a glittering pocket watch with a chain to match. I saw this happen several times and then, with my last shilling, I tried my luck. When two tie pins and two collar studs were unwrapped, I learned my lesson. It is good to realize that you do not get anything for nothing in this life. But by and large we still got our money's worth at those old fairs, in happy memories as well as in more fleeting mementoes such as coconuts, goldfish in jars, favours to decorate our coat lapels, cheap jewellery and ornaments for the mantelpiece, survivors of which you occasionally see at antiques markets today carrying tags of several pounds.

Not that you had to wait for the fair to find something going on in the streets of Evesham. I am not suggesting that they were forever a riot of sights and sounds, but the town of today seems to me the poorer without the newspaper sellers with the *Sports Argus* late on Saturday nights, Alan Hardy's fish stall outside the Town Hall and Mr Staites' barrow of fresh vegetables beside what used to be Timothy White's. I recall, too, a man with a voice like a town crier who went by the name of Freddie Whisper and sold crockery in the Market Square, tossing whole tea services up in the air and clinking porcelain cups hard together to prove their strength. Then there were the scissor grinders and hurdy-gurdy men who stayed overnight at Mr Daffy's lodgings; there was an old tale of a shopkeeper who spoke out strongly against Britain's involvement in the Boer War, and some Evesham folk are said to have paid one of the hurdy-gurdy men to play the stirringly patriotic 'Soldiers of the Queen' outside his premises.

Most memorable of all, though, was Cakey Andrews or Kick Pudding, an Evesham barrow boy from Bengeworth, over the great divide of the Avon river bridge. By and large, the Bengeworth folk were a race apart, and they kept to their patch. Battles were fought on Saturday nights between opposing tribes from Evesham and Bengeworth,

The colour, noise and bustle of the fair were exciting after a long year's labours in the field

a mere six hundred years after Simon de Montfort's more famous conflict near by. Cakey had apparently been a schoolmaster. I gather that at some stage he had been crossed in love and turned very religious, drifting from denomination to denomination. He was no mean orator, and listened intently to the utterings of the Salvation Army, and he always gave the impression of being a true authority on the Bible. And what did he sell? Lardy cakes and bananas, nothing more, nothing less. He would sell them from an iron-wheeled basket truck roughly the size of a supermarket trolley, and his cry of 'Ripe bananas' was the sum total of his salesmanship. He made the lardy cakes himself in a little bakehouse of sorts.

Cakey had studied Darwin's theory of evolution, gradually forsaking his religious beliefs and his teaching to become more of a street politician. He was an ardent woman-hater, and would shock anyone who did not already know his outspoken views. I cannot imagine that this was particularly good for trade, at a time when it was very much the housewife's job to do the shopping, but I never presumed to question him about it. 'Women are deceitful above all things, and desperately wicked,' he would rant. This was just one of his outbursts as he stood leaning over his truck and watching the world go by in the Evesham of the 1920s. I often bought bananas from him.

'How much?' I would ask.

'Two for two-and-a-half,' he replied, and that always irritated me a bit, because half the time I wanted just the one. Looking back, I rather like the reckoning, and would happily go back to tangling with Cakey for my bananas, rather than buying them by the pound in the supermarket. For years Cakey Andrews paraded up and down Bridge Street, and in his home patch of Bengeworth he would occasionally knock on people's doors with his 'two for two-and-a-half' routine if his barrow was still laden after a hard day on the streets. The last time I saw him he was walking along Waterside, outside the old workhouse. It did not seem the most promising territory for his wares, but he never appeared to let that kind of consideration worry him.

CHAPTER ELEVEN

November

Timber in the Grate

A grim month on the land, November, but it was a great time for the social life of the village, and I always looked forward to the get-togethers at the chapel then. The singing and the violin playing around the piano under the recreation room oil lamps did a lot to brighten the dullness of the weather outside, and while simple games like A Hunting We Will Go, Sir Roger and Clap and Run seem pretty feeble in the era of computerized shoot-outs, they suited us well enough in the 1920s. Then there was a memorable Handel's *Messiah*, a long way from the beautiful, uplifting music you hear from some of today's massed choirs and orchestras. Once, I recall, part of it was sung in the recreation room by about fifteen people from a neighbouring village who came to raise money to build our chapel. A man off the land gave his best rendering of 'The Trumpet Shall Sound' on a battered cornet with several holes in the horn filled up with Sunlight soap. His father played a fiddle, an instrument then much discussed because of the performances of a child prodigy named Yehudi Menuhin, but when I say I remember the old man's performance to this day, you need not necessarily take it as a compliment. The lady who took the soprano lead wore a hat with the brim over her eyes; when she sang the top notes she raised her head and the headgear somehow seemed to help carry her up towards roughly where she wanted to go. I still admire the way these good people were prepared to give it their all. By today's standards their performance might have been imperfect; it is a good thing, of course, to hear music produced with perfection, but in those days before compact discs and stereo radio the little local choir fulfilled a real need, and when we all sprang to our feet for the 'Hallelujah Chorus' it was with the kind of gusto that threatened to raise our corrugated iron roof.

The village shop, around which so much of local social life revolved

But oh, the weather. People always quote Thomas Hood's poem *November*, and while I do not think he meant it to be taken too seriously – he was best known in his own time, in the early years of the last century, as a writer of comic songs – I believe there is some truth in his words:

> No sun, no moon, no morn, no noon,
> No dawn, no dusk, no proper time of day.
> No shade, no shine, no butterflies,
> No bees, no fruits, no flowers
> No leaves, no birds, November.

He was writing a century before my childhood in the countryside, but his words are a reminder of how much, even in my early days, we relied upon nature to cheer and uplift us – the sunshine, the birds' song, the cooling shade of the trees. Not that there was much call for the latter in November, for there is so little power in the rays of the sun at this time of year, to the extent that if it does shine, the countryside lies in mist from dawn until it eventually peeps through at noon. Then it is as pale as the moon, as if the moon has taken on the face of what I have heard men on the farm call Bright Famous, a lovely descriptive name. When the mist has cleared, the brief blaze of colour on the trees brightens what is left of the day. Some herbs still flower – groundsel, shepherd's purse – and the gorse goes on bearing some blossom. Toadstools and puffballs spring up among the fallen leaves, yellow, brown, pink and white. Goldfinches flock together and feed on thistle heads. The browns, reds and greys of the ploughlands can please us with more understated colour in the pale sunlight, and there is animation in the hordes of wood pigeons newly in from the Continent to winter on sprouts and kale. No wonder we cling to bonfire night, using old Guy Fawkes as an excuse to bring warmth and colour into our lives. These days the event is hemmed around by Government health warnings, and a good thing, too, but I remember in my village how Jim Huins used to load and reload his muzzle-loader gun and fire it, just to please us boys. The smoke from the black powder was choking for a while, and the flash of the discharge leapt from the gun barrel as a tongue of flame.

The common-or-garden everyday winter fires were another preoccupation come November, and the month was a busy one for our village coal man, even though the wise cottager bought his usual amount of coal all through the summer, so that the stock piled up for use in the colder months; many people still practise the same principle today, spreading their electricity or gas bills over equal monthly instalments. Not that my father always used the coal man; I remember that on one occasion he bought a ten-ton truck load, which was shunted into the little siding of our branch line station. It took our carter a number of journeys with the horse and dray to bring it the last half-mile up the road to our coal house. I can still picture him unloading the dray, shovelling the coal into a pot hamper and carrying it in. Some of the lumps of this hand-hewn fuel were so big that he had to carry them individually; many of them weighed half a hundredweight or more. Not that coal was the only fuel, of course, out in the country. I remember one man in our village who never walked home from the fields on winter evenings without carrying a log for his fire, and the familiar ring of a cross-cut saw sounded especially clear on a frosty day. The farm workers used to tell me that they had the benefit of getting warm twice – once when they sawed the wood, and again when they sat in front of it as it burned in their hearths.

A friend of mine once told me that he would just as soon have a load of hawthorn logs as a load of coal. It is true, hawthorn does burn to a nicety, but ash wood is one of the few that goes up well when it is green. Withy and walnut wood both spit and shower sparks on the rug, while elm wood is said to 'domber' well – a good old country word for smoulder. Never burn elderberry wood, I was told, or the devil will come down your chimney. But I risked it, once, with reasonable results, and if I was visited by Old Nick, he must have been in a lump of soot! There were other dodges, too, far more imaginative than burning coal or wood. When the sprout stems of the Vale of Evesham were eaten down by folded sheep to within nine inches of the ground, the hard lower stems were dug up with the roots and carted into heaps in the corner of the field where they dried hard all the summer. These stems made useful fuel for many a working man's fire. Village women would carry the stems home in their aprons, and I knew one who used to fire her copper boiler for the Monday wash with sprout stems as fuel. Village folk also used to tell me how they banked the fire up with cider pommace, or pommy, as they called it. This consisted of the compounded apple husks from the press, which dried like peat and indeed gave you a good slow burn.

It often makes me laugh, these days, when people say how they cannot wait to leave their centrally heated offices or factories and come home to a real fire in the grate. But I know what they mean; central heating could scarcely be a more clean and convenient way of warming a room, but a coal or wood fire is a living thing – and it is company. I love these words, written by a hand unknown to me, long ago:

> Outside fall the snowflakes lightly;
> Through the night loud raves the storm.
> In my room the fire glows brightly,
> And 'tis cosy, silent, warm.
> Musing sit I on the settle
> By the firelight's cheerful blaze.
> Listening to the busy kettle
> Humming long-forgotten lays.

Life was rather less cosy than this out on the land; when the wheat had been planted, the stubble left from the harvest was dressed with yard muck from the steaming heaps or buries on the headland. It had been carted from the yards and cattle pens on wet days, and here on the buries the toadstools grew like upturned saucers shining white. The old, useful farm cart with its tipping bed is seen no more, but it was so handy to back under the low roofs of the eighteenth-century cattle sheds and load with manure. Those self-same carts drew out from the fields to the roadway on wet November days with hampers of sprouts for market – and I suppose that dual purpose would be something else that would attract a Government health warning these days.

This was the time of year when our forefathers were doing their best to feed themselves up for the winter, to nourish and sustain themselves; this was no self-indulgence but a vital precaution in those days when cold and hardship were never very far removed from the winter

Sharp practice – with even a side-line in repairing umbrellas

doorstep. Bread, cheese and cider could see you very adequately through a hot summer's day, but come November it was time for more substantial fare, if you could manage it. Fat bacon was the staple meat, and that could smell and taste superb when you had a hunger on you. But the roast beef of old England was the real stuff, and if the men of the land and their families could beg, steal or borrow a slice or two of that, it was riches indeed. The fashion at the turn of the century was for beef with plenty of fat on it. The prize beasts at the big Christmas fairs were invariably coated in thick yellow swathes of it that would not be a pretty sight to modern eyes, and indeed were not universally admired at the time. The fat our fathers ate no longer tempts the housewife into the butcher's, but still finds some kind of sale on the Continent. Then, again, there is our current fad for tender meat, and I often wonder how we would have taken to a six-year-old bullock roasted in grandfather's day, for Longhorns and Herefords would pull the plough for four years before they were slaughtered. Bullock teams were a common sight a hundred or more years ago, and it was these faithful beasts of the furrow that ended up as beef in the shops. Tough, was it? No one remembers, now, but I know my grandfather died with a full set of teeth.

In those days, beef was hung in a whole carcase for some time, and then roasted on a spit in front of a wood fire. The dripping would be plastered on chunks of home-made bread, and I remember that before the days of paid holidays on the land, farm workers on some of the estates were given joints of beef and basins of dripping round about Christmas, after parties at the big house. You can read reports of Christmas Day at the workhouse, when the master or mayor carved the beef; and an old friend of mine used to tell me of the delights of his Sunday morning breakfast, which consisted of home-cured bacon, an egg and just a sliver of the dinner joint of beef. Yes, we have long had a preoccupation with eating beef and steak, investing in it a symbolism that goes far beyond the food value of the meat. It somehow speaks of a sense of well-being and a source of physical strength, and those Berni brothers of Bristol knew just what they were doing in the 1960s when, with the return of prosperity after the war, they turned the pursuit of eating steak into a long-lasting national fad. They were simply echoing the spirit of 1709 when the first beefsteak club was formed, the fare being restricted to beer or wines and steaks. In 1735 the Sublime Society of Steaks was founded by John Rick and Lord Peterborough at Covent Garden Theatre, and attracted many famous people, and from then on beefsteak clubs grew and grew in popularity. Another was founded by Sheridan in Dublin in 1749, and yet another by a Stuart Workley in 1875.

In a year of relative prosperity, then, the butcher would expect to enjoy a busy November – and the same could be said for the keeper of the village shop, already stocking up with oranges, nuts and sticky blocks of dates, ready for the Christmas rush. If we were to peep into a shop of the 1920s, before there were buses to take us to the superstore in the nearest town, we would enter a world very different from our own. The shelves in the windows were lined with jars of sweets – acid and pear drops, liquorice and barley sugar – all of them fused together by heat and having to be parted by the white-aproned shopkeeper's wooden spoon when a child asked for four ounces. He would then weigh the sweets on a scale on the scrubbed wooden counter, and make a bag by folding a square of paper into a funnel. For a halfpenny we would buy a bullseye or gobstopper. These hard, round ping-pong balls of sweetness changed colour as they were sucked, and were constantly taken from the mouth for inspection until the last morsel revealed a soft centre.

Shops varied in those days from the more sophisticated store in the next village to Auntie Lucy's front room, where sweets, chocolates and home-made pop could always be found on the table. Apart from that famous drink of hers in Camp Coffee bottles, she also did a line in raspberry vinegar and home-made mushroom ketchup. They talk about the big supermarkets giving us a wider choice than ever before, but try finding those last two commodities on the shelves of Tesco or Safeway today! In shops bigger than Auntie's, looking round would be a real adventure. On the wall, the pocket knives would always take my eye. They were on a card, with the expensive ones at the top, for the shepherd to pare the sheep's feet or the carter to shape whip sticks, while at the bottom, in my price range, were what were called Scout knives, complete with a spike to get stones out of horses' hooves. Paraffin or lamp oil was supplied from a forty-gallon iron drum with a tap. The shopkeeper measured the half gallons of paraffin, and filled the villagers' cans with a dish or funnel. Alongside was the vinegar barrel with its wooden tap to dispense its contents into a variety of receptacles brought in by customers, empty beer bottles being the most common. There was no need to tell people to recycle their glass containers in those days.

The scent from the selection of cheeses was one to remember, and close by was the wire to cut slices off the large chunks. The shopkeeper would cut off wedges about the size of mousetrap bait so that the customer could decide whether it was too mild or too tasty. Tubs and wooden buckets of butter offered a range from the very salty to the only slightly so — and here, again, nothing was wasted, for when the buckets were empty they were sold at sixpence apiece for carrying water. Bacon was cut into rashers with a well-steeled carving knife — slicers were more a luxury reserved for the big town provisions chain stores — and the spin-off in this case was the boxes the meat came in. When fixed to pram wheels, they made good trucks in which to bring the potatoes and other vegetables back from the allotments. A dear old friend in Sedgeberrow used to recall how often she bought two ounces of tea — or even a pennyworth — from the village shop there. It was weighed out straight from the chests of green tea, Darjeeling, Ceylon, whatever the locals liked, and how pretty was some of the paper in which it was wrapped. The empty tea chests were sold for a few coppers, and these made tolerable chicken coops with a few slats of wood in front. It was not until another generation on, in the mid-1950s, that the skifflers discovered that you could make bass fiddles out of them, with the help of a broom handle and a piece of string!

Ground coffee was rarely sold in our village, bottled brands with chicory being the local choice. Cocoa always intrigued me. The well-known brands were said to be pure — an adjective bandied around so much in those days that it ceased to have any real meaning — but for twopence a packet an inferior blend mixed, I recall, with cornflour suited the pockets of many folk who were having a job to make ends meet. All the materials for wash day were at hand in the shop, too — yellow soap in long bars, Hudson's Powder, soda, Reckitt's Blue and white Windsor soap for toilet use. How hard this latter was. A piece would take a long while to wear away, and the lather in our hands was sparse. I

Daily bread – delivered to the door wrapped only in clean, fresh air

doubt if many village folk chew twist tobacco today, or even smoke it, but in the old days it was sold to farm workers by the ounce in long shoe-string pieces. 'I don't want to buy your finger, too,' they would growl at Mr Tandy, voicing that constant preoccupation of the inter-war years, centred on the belief that somehow, with the cunning use of rubber bands, light weights or the deft press of a finger, the shopkeeper was out to fiddle you. No doubt it happened, but customers of our village shop knew, deep down, that they would get fair weight, no more and no less. As one of our villagers used to say: 'Right's right and might's might and wrong's no man's right.' There seemed little cause for complaint, either, in the price of Captain Webb matches at three-halfpence for a dozen boxes.

'Everything in season' was the motto of the man who ran the stores. He knew that folk grew their own vegetables, so he did not offer any for sale except for dried peas that had to be soaked. Split peas were also sold at a cheaper price, and they came in useful for soups, stews and broth. Tinned food was not widely used, and though corned beef at fourpence a tin seemed reasonable enough, countrymen who worked with horses were always dubious about its origins! It was more the food of casual workers, the gentlemen of the road, who flocked to our village every summer. Leather laces for workaday boots and cotton ones for Sundays, reels of cotton, cards of needles, candles by the pound, blocks of salt, little blue bags of sugar: all surrounded the shopkeeper as he went about his tasks in between serving customers, from wiping clean his bacon knife to patting the butter and making the impression of a dairy cow on each pound he worked. Some of the larger village shops had huge mahogany-framed mirrors advertising Pear's Soap or Rowntree's Cocoa, and they gave the shop a feeling of spaciousness as they reflected the goods along the opposite wall. I remember that today, when I survey the long, wide aisles of our local supermarket. But most of all I remember the kind of personal service the supermarkets cannot give, and that air of expectation that came over me every time, as a child, when I struggled to push open the village shop's stiff and heavy door and the bell clanged out to herald my arrival to the spruce figure behind the counter.

CHAPTER TWELVE

December

The Night Our Oxen Knelt

When I was a small boy at school we did not start to think about Christmas until very near the end of term. We would break up about a week before the big day, with blancmange and cake for tea and crackers and tinsel decorating the classroom, but I think I learned more about the true spirit of Christmas in the cosy barn in those short winter days towards the end of December. I liked to creep in and watch the cows being milked by Fred the cowman, who sat on a three-legged stool with his head covered by a greasy cap worn backwards. A hurricane lamp slung on a broken plough trace gave a little light for the milking at five o'clock. The hens, perched in rows on the tall hay loader, cackled occasionally when he walked with his three-gallon bucket and poured the warm, creamy milk into a shining five-gallon container. There is a strange, comforting feeling for man and boy to be with cattle tied up to the manger on a cold winter's night: the incessant chewing of the cud, the placid look in the cows' trustful eyes. Life was rather more brisk and earnest the next morning, when Dad and Fred caught the Christmas cockerels one by one under the thatch in an old bull pen. As they were killed I walked with Fred and he hung them up on hooks and nails from the whitewashed ceiling of the back kitchen. Soon Mrs Vale was busy plucking their feathers into a galvanized bath, being careful to save the breast plumage to stuff pillows.

At just turned six o'clock in the morning on St Thomas's Day, the shortest day, I sat up in bed and heard the familiar chant:

> Here we come a' Thomasin', a' Thomasin', a' Thomasin'
> Here we come a' Thomasin', so early in the morning.

Two or three small boys were at the front door, and the bells were ringing across the Vale from the church, where five shirt-sleeved men off the land, Ralph, Frank, Charlie, Tom and Len were busy at the ropes, their exertions illuminated by a hurricane lamp hanging from a plough trace in the ringing chamber. The boys came to welcome in Christmas early on 21 December, and to collect pennies for their trouble. In other parishes the homes of the local squires, lords of the manor and major farmers would be descended upon on St Thomas's Day, and the estate workers and their families would be treated to refreshments and presents. The custom was known as mumping – a polite term for begging – and in Beckford, for instance, the women and children of the neighbouring hamlet of Grafton would do the rounds, again reciting traditional verses. That did not happen at our farm, but Dad was what was known as a Guardian of the Poor, and he and his partner gave rabbits to Evesham Workhouse every Christmas to enable the people then referred to as inmates, but now more fittingly remembered as patients, to have a rabbit pie supper. We would spend a day up by the parish quarry on Bredon Hill, Dad, a neighbour, my brother Tom and I, ferreting the holts for rabbits.

Christmas drew near. In those days the season seemed more of a festival, more acute, when everything was to happen in a few short days. The village boys shinned up apple trees cutting sprigs of mistletoe, and the cottage doors were hung around with laurel, ivy and yew branches. The furnace in the washroom no longer boiled the sheets and shirts, but Christmas puddings. They simmered away for hours in basins covered in cloths tied down with string. In the Japanese lantern-lit window of Mr Tandy's shop I saw long netting stockings, each with a Father Christmas sitting at one end and a sugar mouse peeping through the mesh. There were boxes of chocolates wrapped in fancy paper, with Father Christmas in business once more, this time decorating the pink ribbons; and there were dishes of muscatels and almonds, sugar mice and Christmas cards. Standing outside, by the door, was a Christmas tree in half a nine-gallon barrel. And when I went to post letters and buy stamps, for the shop also doubled up as a post office, I would watch parcels being weighed on the shining brass scales. As for Christmas Eve, there was a magical time when I still half-believed in Father Christmas – and one year I even saw him walk in through the front door, in the guise of Dad dressed in mother's red dressing gown on his way from Mr Tandy's shop, laden with good things to fill our stockings. He would have collected a gift of his own there, too, for it was the custom of grocers in those days to reward regular customers with some kind of present, perhaps a box of biscuits or some sweets. I say I still half-believed in Father Christmas. Today I have come full circle and believe in him completely, for he is real and represents all that is kind, neighbourly and generous in the world. 'Now is the ancient feud forgot, the growing grudge is laid aside.' These are not idle words, for at this time every year quite ordinary folk are that much kinder, willing for once to go that extra mile.

One year St Thomas's Day was so warm that Charlie Moore, the hurdle-maker who was the captain of the bell ringers, grumbled that he had known colder June days. Tustin, who was going from door to door with Taylor's coal dray, delivering sacks of fuel and dispensing the 'charity coal' for the poor, was equally unimpressed. 'It's a weather breeder,' he pronounced. 'It's no good to us, dost know? We shall have some snow afore the new year.' The sprout pickers in the Vale moved shirt-sleeved among the rows of Brussels, filling their hampers for the Christmas trade. At three o'clock, when the men left the fields for home, Shepherd Tidmarsh turned his weather eyes from Spring Hill to the Cotswold Edge and stood awhile puffing blue smoke from his pipe. 'We be in for a reamer tonight,' he said to Frank and me as we strode down the hill carrying a couple of rabbits we had shot with our number three garden gun. 'It'll freeze like big guns tonight. Just hark at that train at the station, hark how holla it sounds; and my sheep lies uneasy anant the wall.' As the sun set behind the Malvern Hills, as big as a waggon wheel and as red as a September Pearmain, the grass trod crisp under our feet; and at dusk I walked through the young orchard with the shepherd and watched him turn over the iron sheep troughs ready for the morning feed. The rails clung slightly to his gnarled hands as the frost began to ice over the damp metal. 'Tell yer Dad I'll bring the ewes down off the hill tomorrow,' he said. 'It's a bit handier for the hay ricks because I'm tellin' yer, we be in for some unkind weather.'

Next morning the puddles of roadside water were glazed over with ice. I met the shepherd with his flock as they journeyed on their way to the young orchard. The ice-covered grass was cutting their feet, and the white rime or hoar-frost was speckled with blood from their tender cloven hooves, their clays, as we called them. One ewe that had taken the ram early was left on the hill, and we went with Alf Tidmarsh to fetch her down. One of the men drove the milk float up the steep slope, through the gulley between the limestone rocks. The ewe was licking a new-born lamb under the wall, and the little creature was struggling ungainly to its feet, fumbling to find its mother's teats. 'Her's had a rough time, look yer,' said the shepherd, pointing with his crook to something Frank and I had never seen before. It was a lamb encased in ice, like a cocoon of glass. Apparently the ewe had given birth to twins; the first-born had been neglected as she laboured with the second, and a sleet storm in the night had frozen the lamb in the early hours. That afternoon hordes of pigeons swept on to the frozen sprout tops for a late dinner, while droves of hungry larks were busy ragging the glazed cabbage plants. In twenty-four hours winter had come with a vengeance.

Feathers flew when the task of plucking the Christmas fowl came around

Tustin's face shone as the many local vintages of home-made wine were sampled as he delivered the Christmas coal. The snow fell steadily, and he announced that everybody's garden looked tidy. 'My hoss unt happy, though,' he would add. 'I'll have to have him roughed.' Archie the blacksmith was well used to performing this task at this time of year, fitting the horses' shoes with frost nails. 'About time Master Taylor bought you a lorry for pottering around these roads,' the smith re-marked, realistic enough to realize that he would be the last generation of his trade to make a living out of horses alone. 'Mind you, you're too drunk to drive at the moment, anyway. Started Christmassin' early, old butt? Thou cosunt walk straight. Thou canst tell a mon as can't carry his drink a mile away. Him's got crooked stockings on.'

At school, Miss Morris had taught us poems about Christmas. We sang 'Who Is He In Yonder Stall?' among other carols, and when we heard the story of the manger it is hardly surprising that the stable at Bethlehem was transformed in my mind to our barn, complete with Fred and his three-legged stool. Nothing has changed, I thought. The shepherd still watched his flocks by night, but he watched the ewes in the lambing pen, too. Miss Morris also had my rapt attention when she read us a then very new poem by Thomas Hardy, *The Oxen*, written in the West Country in the year I was born. That is the one that begins 'Christmas Eve and twelve of the clock', and harks back to the old country belief that oxen kneel in their stalls at midnight on Christmas Eve. Hardy, by then an old man writing at the height of the First World War, concludes that few people would believe such a fanciful tale in modern times, but confesses that if someone were to invite him out to the cattle shed to investigate:

> I would go out with him in the gloom
> Hoping it might be so.

And that is just what I did one Christmas, creeping out at twelve o'clock to see for myself. In the cattle shed four oxen and two heifers were chained to a manger, and the light from the candle lantern shone on their white faces. The oxen were lying in the straw, and their forefeet were doubled under their briskets in a kneeling position as they comfortably chewed their cud. Taking the lantern back to the house, I was satisfied.

I suppose we felt it was some kind of a miracle, too, the Christmas Eve we had our first wireless set, and the dance band tunes and festive jokes and a reading from *A Christmas Carol* came surging and crackling through the ether from London. So we sat by the black-leaded grate burning a log, and when we turned the set off we were transported back to our own world of the Vale by the church bells, which had been rung for Christmas every week since Guy Fawkes Night in a local tradition stretching back two hundred years or more. We stayed up late and it seemed a dream to me, those festivities of midwinter. But not so much as on the following morning, when I discovered that Santa Claus had remembered me again, and the sweets, the sugar mouse and the orange all bulged the stocking. By now our house was decorated with holly, ivy and mistletoe. Every picture was festooned with greenery, the old grandfather clock was hung with holly and a bough of mistletoe was fixed to a big nail by the front door. Early callers to the village were the Tewkesbury drum and fife band, who played just one carol, 'Oh Come All Ye Faithful'. We called them the Tabber and Tut band, and they were always compared unfavourably with the Salvation Army players. Two little red-faced chaps led a blind man through the village, hoping for the Christmas spirit to reach the hearts of more fortunate folk and fill their collecting box. And a hurdy-gurdy man often followed this little caravan of folk who braved the weather to remind us that Christmas was near. Ponto, who lived rough in the cart house, would give us a rustic rendition of 'Wild Shapperds Watch', in return for some of our Christmas fare in the kitchen, and it was on one such occasion that he came across jelly for the first time. He took to it pretty well. 'I'd like some more of that shaky tack, Ma'am,' he told my mother, before wishing us all the compliments of the season and going on his way. It was sad to think he finished his days at the old workhouse in Evesham.

Christmas breakfast was much as usual – and when I say that, I mean that it was lashings of eggs and bacon, notwithstanding the feasting to come; by ten o'clock the first of many mince pies would be on the table hot from the oven, and at dinner time the Light Sussex cockerel went down well with the vegetables, yet more pies and pudding. Dad had a great say in cooking the bird, carving it with a bone-handled carving fork and basting it in its juices, and it was he who dictated that we should dine on Light Sussex, perhaps cross-bred with Rhode Island, rather than the goose to which some of our neighbours aspired. Goose was not easily digested, said Dad; the cockerel, fed on boiled potatoes and sharps, was much more easy on the stomach.

As the light faded at tea time we walked to our neighbour Harry Bailey's house, where jellies of all shapes and sizes twinkled in the lamp-light on a big dining table under the holly and mistletoe. But jellies were only the tip of the wobbly iceberg; there was ham off the bone, crisp celery – Harry grew a pink variety in his kitchen garden – masses of mince pies, with real mincemeat made from Bittersweet apples from a local orchard, strong, sweet tea and a castle-shaped chocolate blanc-mange with a moulded lion on top. Equally memorable were the shad-ows from the Aladdin oil lamp on the window blinds, and the crackling of burning logs. After we had pulled the crackers, Harry came into the dining room with a peck basket of walnuts from trees in the rick yards, and producing a brass counter like a spinning top, he said to Dad: 'Your first spin, Tom.' Meanwhile, all the party had been served with about twenty walnuts each, with some spare ones in the middle. As the counter came to rest on the table with one of its legends uppermost – perhaps 'Put Two' – Dad put two of the nuts to join the heap in the middle. The game of Put And Take was under way. Sometimes the counter would read 'Take All', and the lucky player would win the lot. A feeble game? Not at all – not in that happy company, in those days long before television had taken over our Christmas celebrations. Another game was Pit; the cards were dealt and we strove to collect enough of one variety to claim a corner as we exchanged Wheat, Oats, Barley, Beans and Rye across the table. When a set of one variety of cereals was in hand we shouted: 'Corner on barley!' or 'Corner on Rye!' What a game! What a party! After singing a few carols around the piano, it was time for my parents to take us sleepy little ones home. There in the hall beside the grandfather clock the box of Tom Putt or Nine Square apples and sack of oranges for the carol singers had grown lighter, and as I drifted off to sleep I wondered how the rabbit pie sup-per had been enjoyed at the workhouse. The workhouse system was

Mistletoe in the old snug: little boys would risk life and limb to cut sprigs of the parasite to sell to neighbours

indefensible, and the Christmas Day In The Workhouse scene described in the poem by George R. Sims, the nineteenth-century social re-former, was a scathing indictment of it, even though endless comic parodies have lessened his verses' impact on later generations. They were Public Assistance Institutions and a little more liberal by the time I knew them, and all I know is that the food for those rabbit pie suppers was provided by us with good heart and in good faith. I do wonder how much the extra food at Christmas compensated for the hard rations of the rest of the year, and the condescension of the 'betters' at some of the meals must indeed have been hard to bear. But when once I went to a rabbit pie supper, it was good to see the beams on some of the faces I knew.

Christmas to me was not complete until the Salvation Army band vis-ited the village to play carols, gathering at the cross to regale us with wonderful and timeless tunes like Hark the Herald Angels Sing, melodies that sent the heart soaring and lightened the winter's gloom. To hear the Salvationists on a crisp, frosty night was magic. Then the bell ringers came and sang around a hurricane lamp hung on a bean pole. The best of their singers with his rich, deep bass voice was Frank Whittle, who went on crutches after losing a leg in the Great War. In spite of this disability he was a great walker, and could always be seen following the Croome Hounds on one leg after Christmas. I once went with him on one of these occasions, and it was all I could do to keep up with him as he took massive strides on his crutches. The ringers were seen as by far the pick of the carol singers; but well primed they were, one night, bless them, and when their faltering version of 'While Shepherds Watched', to the less familiar tune of Lyneham, finally ground to a halt with the line 'Begin and never cease', Dad could not resist telling them: 'It would be a bad job if you chaps began and never ceased.' In retrospect, I wonder about that. They have ceased, now, but they will never be forgotten by me, and the words of a local carol and their plain truth ring in my ears much as they did when they spilled out of the lips of those half-dozen good men and true:

> Behold, the bounteous gift of heaven
> This day to all mankind is given;
> Oh, happy day, mankind rejoice,
> And praise Him with a cheerful voice.

They tramped the lanes around the village with their carols for days around Christmas, those ringers, and in memory there is something almost haunting about their voices proclaiming the tidings of joy in the clear, still air. But of course in real life they were country chaps who worked hard and enjoyed a drop like a million others, and never did they enjoy a drop more than at their annual supper, which was always looked forward to as a good do, with roast beef on the menu and thick heads the following morning. I remember Ralph telling me about one he had been to the previous night, where the vicar had started on his beef when the churchwarden was still carving. 'Hadn't we better say grace, Vicar?' the warden had asked, and it had been with some embarrassment that the man in black had sought belated blessings on the meat and pickles and apple pie. Wiry little Ralph was a long-serving ringer, and that year he had asked along the shepherd Alf Tidmarsh as his guest, just so that he could sing his song:

She was sixteen stone, all muscle and bone,
And she looked with an awful leer,
She would have been mine
But she fell into decline
Through swallowing a mouse in her beer.

Then they had had more fun with the parson, said Ralph: 'In his speech he said he would like to see the bell ringers in church more often, and up jumped the captain of the tower, Charlie Moore the hurdle maker, him as rings the tenor bell. He'd had a few drinks and he replied: "Oi, and I ud like to see the parson up the tower sometimes." Then, when we had had about as much as we could eat, the doctor in the chair asked if anyone would like any more food. "Yes, me," I said, and they all stared until I added: "Tomorrow." Then I got up and sang my song.'

We were ploughing at the time, and he sang it to me in his mellow voice not in that smoke-filled room but out on the broad winter acres:

I love green fields, I love the sunshine,
The robin with pretty red breast.
I love pussy cat fast asleep on the mat,
But I love my dear mother the best.'

My Uncle Jim was another man who could tell a good story, and one he always delighted in was his tale of Christmas 1890, when he and a friend of his called Austin Stephens were employed by the eccentric and reclusive Squire William of Ashton-under-Hill, who did not celebrate on 25 December like the rest of us but observed the old Christmas Day of 6 January. He employed most of the men and boys in the village, and though some of them went to work on two sticks, his philosophy was: 'I've had the best out of you, and now I'm prepared to take the worst.' It must be said that there was some method in his madness in this respect; as the village's biggest ratepayer by far, he would have had to foot the lion's share of the bill if the men had gone on parish relief. In other respects, there seems to have been little method in his madness. Imagine a squire who sharpened ducks' beaks to encourage them to peck up their food like hens. Imagine a squire who ordered that his dogs should be given cider one cold winter's day, saying they looked 'starved to death'. Imagine a squire who told the coal man: 'No, I don't want any more; we had to burn the last lot.' Then there was the time he heard that to prevent pigs from getting swine fever, it was necessary to cut their tails and ears slightly. He persuaded the cowman to hold the creatures while he did the job, slicing a fair bit off their ears in particular. The servant did not like it and protested: 'If I were you, gaffer, I wouldn't cut so much off their ears.'

'You shut up or I'll serve you the same,' Squire William retorted.

My uncle's parting from the squire's employment was scarcely less eccentric. Although we have noted that Squire William was a great employer of lame ducks, there was nothing infirm about Uncle Jim and his pal Austin back in 1890. They were strapping young lads, well capable of carrying sacks of wheat weighing two-and-a-quarter hundredweight from the steam-driven threshing machine that was the squire's pride and joy. One morning the men were threshing wheat in the barn when he looked in and caught them at 'bait' time, sitting around eating their mid-morning snack while the threshing drum stood silent. 'Get those wheels turning,' he ordered Fireman Davis, who obediently restarted the engine. Soon the belt was flapping again, and the drum was calling its familiar 'more, more, more'. No sheaves were fed into the machine, but the sight of turning wheels and the chuff, chuff, chuff of the engine satisfied the squire. That evening, Uncle Jim asked for a rise in his wages of ten shillings a week.

'You're getting more money now than you deserve,' the squire replied.

'Ah, but we're carrying the sacks while the other men are only able to do very little,' retorted Uncle Jim. That simply prompted the squire to come out with his usual line about taking the best and worst of the men, which he saw as a justification for paying everyone a flat nine or ten shillings. But then he came up with an extraordinary offer, taking scores of gold coins from his leather purse and presenting them to the youth, along with his rifle and cartridges, saying:

'Here, Jim, a hundred sovereigns and my gun if you'll go and shoot the village doctor.' Not surprisingly, Uncle Jim and Austin left the squire's employment after that. They walked around Bredon Hill that Christmas, Jim playing his melodion while his friend sang the carols, and they cleared more apiece than they would have earned in a month from the squire.

They left Squire William, however, with a host of memories. Uncle Jim had been under-cowman at the Manor, and one of his jobs was to drive the milking cows from a field known as Tun Flun or Ten Acres to Middle Farm. One evening he was riding an old roan Shorthorn cow from the fields when he met the squire. 'Ah, Jim boy,' said the old man. 'I'll have to get you a hoss to ride.' On Christmas morning the men who looked after the animals – the carter, the shepherd, the cowman and Uncle Jim – had their breakfast in the big kitchen of the Manor, fat boiled bacon, home-baked bread and plenty of cider being the order of the day. 'Here, Jim,' the squire said after the meal. 'Come and test the cider in the big barn.' So they went and they tested it, barrel after barrel, until in the end my uncle did not know whether the drink was good, bad or indifferent. There then followed an odd game in which the squire half-filled a long bath with port, and Uncle Jim was commissioned to catch four drakes off the pond and put them to one end of it. All the stockmen sat around it and laid bets on which of the birds would swim to the other end first, until eventually the squire grew tired of this sport, my uncle was told to take the drakes back to the water and the men were urged to drink the port from the bath. 'Now I'll sweep the chimney,' the squire declared, and taking his gun he fired several shots up the flue, bringing down a cloud of dust and soot. Uncle later told me that two male nurses from London, known as the squire's keepers, had taken the shot from the cartridges.

What a Christmas that was at the Manor. And there were some strange times to follow, for not long afterwards the squire was found sitting in a wheelbarrow in the middle of the shallow moat pond, saying he was fed up with England and was off to America. He died peacefully some time later, sitting beside his keepers in a horse-drawn trap in a lane near the village, and the sale of his effects was still being talked of when I was a boy. He had a score or more of unbroken cart horses up on Bredon Hill – he bought them at market at often ridiculous prices and made no attempt to harness them, saying he just liked to see them around – and how they were handled in the sale in the church close is beyond my imagination; they had never had a collar on in their lives. Among his many bulls there was a savage white Shorthorn, and he apparently made his mark on the proceedings, too. Never was there a farm sale like the squire's!

The last highlight on the seasonal calendar was the chapel Sunday school Christmas tea and social. Here in the recreation room under the corrugated iron roof of this First World War army hut, the joint efforts of Harry Bailey and William Boulton made the party go with a swing. I reckon the adults enjoyed it as much as the children, for they often played what always seemed fairly rough sports. Musical chairs, as I remember, was more like a rugby scrum as the farm lads shoved and pushed and sprawled on the dusty floorboards. As William Boulton's voice grew husky towards nine o'clock, and we settled down to a quiet game of Winking, Harry Bailey came through the door with a waggon rope. We sat with him by the stove while the young men and girls from the farm houses dashed around the circle of chairs and played Clap and Run. Then William took a bunch of keys from his pocket and orga-nized A-Hunting We Will Go. The atmosphere by then was pretty warm. Men's jackets were hung on the coat hooks or laid across the bil-liard table. Then came the *pièce de résistance* as Harry Bailey uncoiled his rope, which stretched the length of the room. Two sturdy men of the land picked their teams, and here in this old army hut a genuine tug-'o-war took place. As heavy boots slid along the floorboards and one team and then another held sway, we cheered our group on. At one point the rope broke, catapulting one team on to the stage and the other against the door. By now the younger children had gone home, clutching their presents. Some had scored fifty-two marks for full Sunday school atten-dance during the year, a feat announced by Father Christmas, alias William Boulton. They took with them, besides their presents from the Christmas tree, oranges, apples, and more of Harry Bailey's walnuts. Then the waggon rope went back to the barn until haymaking time.

And that is how we celebrated the Nativity in a village that could just as well have been a moated castle at Christmas time. No one left, and very few folk came. There was a feeling of self-sufficiency, and the sea-son fostered a community spirit that lasted the whole year through. We learned as children to use the things around us for pleasure, the pig's bladder as a football, the old drill wheels as hoops. Looking back, now, that first Christmas with a wireless set was not so much a novelty as a foretaste of the future, our introduction to an outside world of seemingly endless entertainments and glittering temptations. Before we knew it, the pattern of life in our village that had changed so little 'since Adam was a bwoy' would be lost to us forever.